In The Arms Of

Gitche Gumee

The Political Journey Of
Evangeline LeBlanc

JAMES P. HILL

In The Arms Of Gitche Gumee
The Political Journey Of Evangeline LeBlanc

Artwork by Nicholas Hill
Graphics by Patricia Anderson

ISBN 978-1-66785-957-6
ISBN eBook 978-1-66785-958-3

ACKNOWLEDGEMENT AND DEDICATION

My sincere appreciation goes to my dear friend, classmate, and superb author Sue Harrison, whose expert guidance and encouragement made this novel possible.

I also extend my deepest gratitude to my talented brother Nicholas, who created the original artwork for the cover of this book, and for the graphics by my daughter Patricia Anderson, an excellent professional photographer.

Most importantly, I want to thank my loving wife Kathryn, who kept me on course throughout this long, fiction-writing journey. You helped me realize a long-sought dream to write this Upper Peninsula-based political novel, and I dedicate it to you, my love.

The Upper Peninsula of Michigan

CHAPTER ONE

The Longest Wait

Come hither! Come hither! My little daughter.
And do not tremble so;
For I can weather the roughest gale
That ever wind did blow

—*The Wreck of the Hesperus,* Henry Wadsworth Longfellow

GRAND MARAIS, MICHIGAN
NOVEMBER 6, 2007

STANDING ON A SMALL, SANDY BLUFF, A GRIM-FACED, FIRST AMERICAN girl tightly squeezed her sister's hand, gazing at the frenzied activity on the beach below.

Colorfully garbed tribal members rushed to their kayaks in the wake of an approaching storm, hoping to avert its full fury. Stiff winds had shattered the big lake's early morning calm, transforming its glass-like blue water into dark, angry waves.

"Are they leaving without us?" nine-year-old Evangeline LeBlanc shouted, tugging on her sister's hand in frustration as her parents boarded a long canoe and disappeared behind the wildly flapping tribal flags strapped to its sides.

She could hear her father barking orders to the kayakers to line up behind him. The long procession of tribal watercraft created an impressive spectacle for reporters recording the launch from the same bluff.

Wenonah, her older sister, smiled and waved, nudging Evangeline to do the same. But Evangeline remained sullen as she watched her parents' canoe and the kayak flotilla push away from the beach.

"Why can't we go with them?" Evangeline pleaded, staring up at her older sister. "Mommy promised we could."

"Father said it's better if Auntie drives us to the Point," Wenonah replied. Clearing her throat, she continued, "Since the weather is worse than expected."

Evangeline saw her older sister's lips tighten as she finished her sentence.

"Why can't they go tomorrow?" Evangeline persisted.

"Mother and Father spent a lot of time organizing this. Tribal members came from all over to be here today, so they just can't tell them to come back tomorrow."

Evangeline frowned in disagreement.

"And you saw all those people with cameras. They're taking pictures of all this to put in the news," Wenonah further explained.

"But those big, black clouds!" Evangeline protested, pointing to the dark billowing clouds rapidly advancing from the north.

Her Aunt Abequa, who was standing nearby, overheard her niece's questions and offered words of comfort to Evangeline.

"Don't worry, dear," her aunt chimed in. "Your parents are strong canoeists, as is your uncle, who will be right behind them. Your father told me they plan to hug the shoreline to stay safe. They'll get to the Whitefish Point faster if they do, so let's hurry to the car."

Evangeline pushed away her sister's extended hand and headed towards her aunt, who now was walking to her car. Her cousin Frank joined Abequa, and the two walked ahead of the girls to the parking lot.

She was not close enough to hear what the two were saying, as a group of men and women with cameras rushed by her, shouting directions and orders to get to the Point.

She sensed something important was happening, as they were having a very animated conversation.

Maybe I can catch up to them, she thought, and picked up her pace. But before she could reach them, Frank hugged Abequa and pivoted towards his car on the other side of the lot.

"I want to go with Frank," she shouted to her aunt as she tried to follow him, but her aunt frowned and pointed to her car.

"It's not fair," she shouted, as she stomped towards her aunt.

No canoe trip, no breakfast, another long car trip, and now no cousin to talk to on the ride back. Why did I bother to get up so early for this, Evangeline wondered as she yanked open the car door?

Plunking down in the back seat of her aunt's car, she was soon joined by Wenonah. But instead of comforting Evangeline, Wenonah leaned forward and spoke in a hushed voice to her aunt, aware that young Evangeline was within earshot. Though outwardly appearing disinterested, Evangeline strained to hear their conversation.

"How bad do you think the weather will get?" Wenonah whispered to her aunt.

Abequa, signaling concern with her darting eyes that her words might disturb the younger niece, replied that she had heard the worst of the storm would not make landfall until early afternoon, after the flotilla was expected to land at White Fish Point.

"Do you think reporters will still come to the Point? Will their stories about today still make front-page headlines?" Wenonah continued.

"Always the politician looking for headlines," her aunt chuckled. "You are the shrewdest fifteen-year-old I know, Wenonah."

"Well, I know Father wanted a big news splash with the flotilla, so it would be awful if the storm scared them off."

"Don't worry. With this many tribes protesting a foreign corporation trying to steal old Gitche Gumee's water, it is a big news event—storm or no storm," her aunt consoled her.

"Gitche Gumee?" Evangeline interrupted.

Wenonah and Abequa both looked startled, unaware that she had been listening to their conversation.

"That's what Longfellow called Lake Superior," her aunt responded. "It goes by many names, but it means the Great Sea and is what your parents and uncle are trying to protect by this protest."

Evangeline opened her mouth to ask more questions, but her aunt cut her off.

"You are too young to understand all this. We can talk more about this later."

Shut out again, thought Evangeline. I wish she wouldn't treat me like a baby. I'm almost ten years old!

She pulled off her green beaded headband and kicked off her moccasins in frustration. When Wenonah did the same, Abequa delivered a stern rebuke.

"Put your headbands back on!" Abequa ordered. "Your mother spent the better part of two days beading them for you to wear to this launch, and you need to be wearing them when your parents land."

"But Auntie," both sisters responded in unison.

"No buts," Abequa responded. "This is a big day, and you can keep them on just a little while longer."

Wenonah put her moccasins and headband back on and then helped her sister with her headband. But Evangeline's moccasins stayed off.

They both peered out the car window as they left the parking lot in Grand Marais. Trees along the road were now swaying ominously. The bright morning sunshine disappeared as black clouds continued their relentless march towards the shore.

Evangeline hesitated before asking another question, as she could see the clenched jaw of her aunt through the rearview mirror, but she wanted to know what her aunt had told her cousin Frank. Just as she summoned the courage to break the silence, loud static from the car radio interrupted the moment, as her aunt frantically scanned the local radio channels.

"Frank thought the local PBS station would broadcast a recorded interview with your parents at the top of the hour, so I'm trying to find that station," she explained as she fumbled with the radio channel knob. The radio static and abrupt jumping from one station to another annoyed Evangeline. She frowned at her sister as they waited for the noisy interlude to end.

"There it is," her aunt cried out triumphantly, as a station identified itself as the Northern Michigan University Public Broadcasting Station. "Hush now, as your parents' flotilla might be the lead news story."

Sure enough, the radio reporter announced they would begin the hour with a recorded interview with the leaders of the "Save Gitche Gumee" flotilla at Grand Marais, Michigan.

"But first, a live NPR news report from Washington," the newscaster interjected.

Evangeline groaned as the national news reporting droned on, but her sister nudged her to be quiet. Wenonah was very interested in national politics and remarked how happy she was to hear that the education bill being analyzed by the reporter had passed Congress.

"It will be good for rural schools in Michigan," Wenonah declared.

Evangeline rolled her eyes. How could her sister know that?

But Abequa praised Wenonah's interest.

"Wenonah, I hope you go into politics someday. Our country needs more smart women like you."

Evangeline stared at her sister, rolling her eyes in disgust.

Wenonah just smiled.

Then the local news returned with the report they wanted to hear.

"This is John Surrell, reporting from Grand Marais, Michigan. I'm speaking this morning with the leaders of the 'Save Gitche Gumee' protest movement, Arthur and Margaret LeBlanc. Tell me folks, what you are protesting and why here in Grand Marais?"

They listened as Arthur spoke first.

"Well, as you know, the Canadian government received a request to ship large quantities of water out of old Gitche Gumee—what you whites call Lake Superior—to the Far East. There are rumors Michigan received a similar request, and we First Americans are here today to demonstrate to our political leaders our vehement opposition to any such water withdrawal proposal."

Arthur, clearing his throat, continued. "We have assembled a flotilla of twenty-five kayaks representing twenty-five Native American tribes from around the Great Lakes region to bring public attention to this desecration of our freshwater seas. Our lead canoe displays the flags of all twenty-five tribes and will start here, ending at White Fish Point."

(Reporter) "But why here?"

(Margaret responding) "Grand Marais is the gateway to our sacred Pictured Rocks. We think we can reach Whitefish Point from here just before noon, when we will gather on the beach and celebrate our journey and our mission to protect Gitche Gumee."

(Reporter) "November is a dangerous time for boating in Lake Superior. It is the largest and most unpredictable of all the Great Lakes. There is a good reason they call Whitefish Point the graveyard of the Great Lakes, especially in November. Aren't you worried that the weather service has just issued a gale warning for Lake Superior later this morning?"

(Arthur speaking) "We revised our original timetable and are leaving sooner than planned because of the weather threat. We'll hug the Lake Superior shoreline along our route and can take shelter on the beach if the weather gets bad. We're all experienced canoeists and kayakers, so I am confident we can beat the early storm waves."

The reporter continued interviews with other tribal participants, but Abequa turned down the radio and smiled at the girls.

"See, everything will be OK girls. Don't worry."

Evangeline grinned with pride at her sister. How exciting to hear Mommy and Daddy on the radio, she mused.

But as their car turned north towards Whitefish Point, Evangeline cringed as the sky became black with howling wind gusts that shook their car. It seemed more like midnight than mid-morning. Had the storm already arrived, and would Mommy and Daddy be safe?

As if reading her niece's mind, Abequa tuned the radio dial to the weather station to get an update. Wenonah turned to Evangeline and whispered, "Just close your eyes and we'll get to the Point before you know it."

I don't think so, Evangeline thought to herself, but sleeping was preferable to staring at the bad weather and listening to a crackling radio, which now was turned down so low that she couldn't hear the weather updates.

But no sooner had she closed her eyes and dozed into a light sleep than she sensed the car slowing down. Torrents of rain beat on the car roof like golf balls. Evangeline opened her eyes and saw Wenonah leaning forward, pointing at something ahead of them.

"What's wrong?" Evangeline cried, now sitting erect and staring at a blurred windshield that the wipers could barely clear.

Her aunt pulled over to the side of the road, joining the caravan of cars ahead of them. She turned up the radio volume only to hear a chilling weather update for Lake Superior:

"The National Weather Service has issued a revised small craft warning for the eastern portion of Lake Superior. Gale force winds are generating waves of eight to ten feet along the shoreline between Marquette and Whitefish Point. All small craft in this area are strongly advised to take shelter at any harbor of refuge or beach. Expect waves to crest around noon, Eastern Standard Time. This advisory will remain in effect until 2:00 pm. Stay tuned to this station for further updates on this rapidly developing weather pattern."

Abequa glanced through the rear-view mirror and saw the two girls huddled together in the backseat. Evangeline could see in her aunt's face that the weather report had visibly shaken her, but Abequa assured the girls there was nothing to worry about and that they would stay on the side of the road until the rain subsided.

After nearly twenty minutes, the pelting rain eased, and Abequa pulled back on the road and resumed their journey north towards Whitefish Point. When they arrived at the small town of Paradise, about eleven miles south of Whitefish Point, she stopped and parked in front of a general merchandise store.

"Wait here while I try to find some rain gear for us," she instructed the girls. "I'll be right back."

Evangeline watched as her aunt dashed into the store and returned in a few minutes with a small bag.

Abequa jumped in and tossed the bag to Wenonah.

"There were no ponchos or rain gear left. The reporters ahead of us bought them out. So, I bought some large garbage bags to wear when we get to the beach."

"Garbage bags? I'm not wearing a garbage bag over my new clothes," Evangeline protested.

"Hush," Abequa scolded, as she put the car in gear and proceeded on their trip to Whitefish Point.

Evangeline tried to make eye contact with Wenonah, who stared straight ahead and smirked.

* * *

The last few miles to the Point seemed like an eternity to Evangeline. The sky had turned pitch black, with gusty winds whipping the evergreen trees like stalks of grain. The long line of cars ahead of them was now moving at a snail's pace. She perched on the edge of her seat, straining to see the tall, white lighthouse that would signal they had reached the Point.

She just wanted to hug her Mommy.

A blurry outline of the lighthouse finally materialized ahead.

"There it is!" Evangeline shouted.

"Sit back, Evangeline," her aunt cautioned. "Let me get us parked."

But when they pulled into the Point parking lot, there was no place left to park. They could hear the waves crashing on the shoreline just beyond the lighthouse, even over the howling northerly wind.

"I thought the storm wasn't supposed to hit shore before noon," Wenonah exclaimed.

Abequa shook her head in confusion.

Wenonah leaned forward and Evangeline saw her whisper something to her aunt, as Abequa desperately searched for any opening in the crowded lot.

Seeing reporters with cameras leave their cars and fight powerful wind gusts to get to the observation deck overlooking the beach, Abequa spotted a uniformed park official vigorously signaling her to keep moving.

She pulled up beside him and rolled down her window.

"Excuse me, sir, but my husband and my niece's parents are part of the flotilla that's landing here, but we can't find a place to park," Abequa pleaded.

The park official leaned in and glared at her and the children in the back seat. Evangeline felt a chill as the official fixed his gaze on her aunt and sneered.

"That's not my problem, ma'am. I can't create a parking space. You people should have come earlier; now move on," the park official sniffed and stood back, waving her forward.

Evangeline could sense her aunt's anger as she repeated his "you people" epithet under her breath.

"We were here long before you were," her aunt shouted before rolling up her window.

"Can't we just get out of the car here?" Evangeline gasped.

"Yeah, let's just get out here," Wenonah shouted in agreement.

Abequa shook her head and made another lap around the parking lot, listening to weather report updates.

Evangeline could only make out the words "gale warning" in the radio weather report.

"What's a gale?" Evangeline asked. But Wenonah and Abequa ignored her question and stared straight ahead in stone-faced silence.

A news bulletin then interrupted the forecast. Evangeline and Wenonah both leaned forward with a report that overturned kayaks had been found west of Whitefish Point and the Coast Guard had launched a rescue mission.

"Mommy!" Evangeline screamed.

"Oh my God!" Wenonah and her aunt both yelled in unison.

Evangeline threw open the rear car door and began running in her bare feet towards the observation deck. She heard her aunt and sister yelling for her to come back, as she dashed against the wind and the drenching rain. She could hear Wenonah's voice getting louder as her sister was gaining in a race to the observation deck, but Evangeline would not stop until she saw the lake.

When she reached the observation deck ramp, Evangeline froze in horror.

Huge, white-capped waves crashed against the beach below, with reporters snapping pictures of the stormy scene.

Wenonah grabbed Evangeline by the arm and began dragging her back down the deck ramp, but Evangeline broke free and ran back up.

Meanwhile, Abequa had abandoned her car in the middle of the lot in a desperate attempt to find her nieces. Joining her nieces on the observation deck, they struggled in vain to see any sign of the flotilla.

A local reporter was attracted to the colorfully dressed but drenched Abequa and approached her for an interview. Although Evangeline continued to stare westward, she listened attentively to his words for any information about her parents.

"Are you concerned some kayakers may have drowned?"

Evangeline saw her aunt glare at the reporter and then turn away from him.

The reporter continued, "Was it a mistake for the flotilla to have launched today?"

Abequa was a large woman, and she appeared even more so standing beside the diminutive reporter. She leaned in towards the reporter and responded in a voice that everyone nearby could hear, despite the thunderous weather.

"The weather wasn't supposed to be this bad, for God's sake!"

The anger in her aunt's voice, usually so calm and comforting, made Evangeline even more fearful of the peril her parents faced.

She tugged on her aunt's arm for attention, but her aunt pulled away her hand and continued to chastise the reporter. Wenonah tried to step between them, but the angry conversation continued.

"My husband and family are out there, and you're scaring the daylights out of my nieces with all of your stupid questions. The men and women in those kayaks are strong, dedicated First Americans who are out there to protect our Big Sea. Gitche Gumee will not forsake them," her aunt declared.

Evangeline felt a rush of pride in her aunt's words. Maybe it was going to be all right after all, she thought.

Then a voice on the deck called out, "Here they come!"

People on the observation deck rushed to the railing to look for signs of the flotilla, and Wenonah raised little Evangeline on her shoulders so she could see over the crowd.

Evangeline saw the outline of several small vessels headed towards them and shouted with joy. But as the first vessels moved closer, Evangeline only saw kayaks.

"I don't see Mommy and Daddy's canoe!" Evangeline shouted.

Wenonah and her aunt urged her to be patient, but Evangeline saw the fear in their eyes despite their words.

"How many kayaks do you see?" one reporter called out.

"I count six!" shouted another.

Six? Did they say six? Evangeline had seen many more leave Grand Marais.

"Where's Mommy and Daddy's canoe?" Evangeline repeated.

"Maybe they landed on a beach farther away," Wenonah replied. But Evangeline was not comforted by the less than convincing tone of her sister's response.

As the six kayaks pulled up to the beach near the deck and their riders jumped out, members of the Coast Guard whisked them away. The small crowd gathered on the railing cheered, but there still was no sign of Evangeline's parents or her uncle.

Seeing no other vessels on the horizon, Abequa grabbed her nieces' hands and marched to the white block building where Coast Guard officers were taking the six kayakers.

She recognized one kayaker and called out to him.

"Did you see my husband or Arthur and Margaret?"

The kayaker shrugged as the Coast Guard officer physically escorted him into the building.

"Does anyone know where the rest of the flotilla is?" Abequa shouted over the din of voices in the crowd, pushing and shoving her way through the crowd and begging to be let in the building and out of the rain.

"My husband and my children's parents were in the flotilla. Please let us in."

But the cluster of reporters and tourists blocked entry into the building and refused to budge, leaving the three drenched in the rain and straining to hear the muffled words of the briefing inside.

The briefing was short, with Coast Guard officials taking no questions and the crowd dispersing after five minutes. Abequa and her nieces stood near the entrance, waiting to approach any of the kayakers as they departed. The one she recognized earlier emerged and spotted Abequa. He made a beeline towards her, despite entreaties by reporters to stop for an interview.

He hugged Abequa and then the girls.

"What happened? Please tell me everyone is safe," Abequa blurted out, forgetting her nieces were listening.

"We were about three miles from Whitefish when the waves got so high they nearly tipped us over. Arthur signaled we should head for shore, but your husband lost his paddle, and a wave flipped his kayak. Arthur turned his canoe around to rescue him and that's the last I saw of them," the kayak survivor related.

"So, they may have gone to the beach after picking up my husband, and that's why they didn't follow you?" their aunt asked hopefully.

Evangeline and Wenonah hugged each other at the possibility.

"I hope so," he responded. "The six of us thought we could make the last few miles to finish our journey and pushed on, but the rest went ashore about three miles west of here."

Abequa hugged the man and then grabbed the hands of her nieces, with the three rushing towards a nearby Coast Guard officer.

"Is a rescue party being sent to the beaches?" asked Abequa.

The officer confirmed a team was being dispatched and was expected to report back with more information within the hour.

A few minutes later, they overheard a reporter telling his colleagues that a helicopter spotted a large group of kayakers on a beach a few miles west of the Point. The three followed the throng of reporters rushing back to the observation deck for more updates.

After waiting and shivering on the observation deck for almost half an hour, Evangeline saw a Coast Guard officer in a wet slicker push his way through the crowd and march to the captain in charge of the rescue. The Coast Guard had roped off the front half of the observation deck to serve as a visual outpost. Everyone ran up to the rope to hear what he had to report. But the two officers moved to the farthest corner of the deck, and the captain signaled to the crowd for silence as he listened to the report.

Evangeline, again hoisted on her sister's shoulders, watched the grim faces of the two men huddled on the deck, sensing it was not good news.

The captain then turned to the small crowd and announced that they had had found most of the kayakers and all were in good health. Then he paused, adding words that were met with stunned silence by all the observers.

"But the lead canoe and one kayak washed ashore without riders. The Coast Guard has already launched a rescue mission to locate the missing riders."

"Was there a name on the empty kayak?" her aunt shouted over the crowd.

"I'm sorry, ma'am, but that's all the information I have," the captain replied.

"It was the 'Hiawatha'," the other officer blurted out.

The captain glared at the officer for contradicting him.

"The empty kayak was named the 'Hiawatha', but that's all I can report," the captain responded. Then he marched off the deck to the temporary communication center in the lighthouse, with the reporting officer following close behind.

Evangeline watched as her aunt's eyes welled up. The "Hiawatha" kayak belonged to Abequa's husband, and the only canoe in the flotilla belonged to the parents of her nieces. Wenonah clung to her aunt, tears flowing down her cheeks.

Evangeline, seeing her two closest companions in sorrow, also burst into tears. A hush came over the surrounding crowd as the reporters snapped pictures of the three sobbing in despair.

Sensing the crowd's reaction, Abequa composed herself, assuring her nieces that both their parents and their uncle were strong swimmers and bravely announcing aloud, "If anyone can survive the waves of Gitche Gumee, they can."

About an hour later, the captain returned to the deck and advised everyone to go home. The Coast Guard had sent rescue teams to the beach area to bring the remaining kayakers to a temporary facility and launched two rescue boats and a helicopter to search for survivors in the water. But these efforts would take time to process, he warned, so there would be no further reports that day.

"Where is the beach area?" Abequa shouted.

"The entire five-mile shoreline west of here, but we have cordoned it off so no one may enter. We don't want spectators hindering our rescue efforts, so everyone please take shelter. We will provide updates online if there are further developments," the captain responded.

"Come, girls, let's get out of the rain and find a motel room while we wait for more news," her aunt coaxed.

"I don't want to leave," Evangeline wailed. "I want to stay here and wait for Mommy and Daddy."

Wenonah put her arms around Evangeline and tried to comfort her, but Evangeline pushed her away. She refused to leave without her parents, so they stayed on the deck while the rest of the crowd departed. A Coast Guard official approached them after everyone else had left and told them they would have to leave, as they were sealing off the observation deck.

Reluctantly, Evangeline left for the parking lot with her sister and aunt. But their car was nowhere to be found, as Abequa had abandoned it in a parking lot lane in her rush to find her nieces. Abequa saw the same park official she had talked to earlier, but he was now directing traffic out of the lot. She approached him, holding on to the hands of her two nieces.

"Excuse me, sir. Have you seen my car?"

"You were the one who just left your car in the middle of the lot, weren't you?" he snarled. "Well, they towed your car to Paradise. Who do you think you are, anyway?"

She tried to explain, but the park official would have none of it.

"I don't care. I have traffic to deal with," he replied and turned his back to her. "You figure it out."

A barefooted Evangeline was now shivering from the chilly rain and wind which had thoroughly soaked them all.

Abequa flagged down a local radio station vehicle. The driver, seeing their desperate situation, gave the three a ride to Paradise. Stuffed in the back of a small van, Evangeline huddled with her sister as they listened to the reporters speculate on the fate of the missing riders.

It was only a twenty-minute drive, but the negative tone of the conversation made the trip seem much longer.

* * *

When they arrived in Paradise, the few lodging facilities in the tiny town had posted "no vacancy" signs. So, the reporters drove to Newberry, many miles further south of the Point. Abequa needed to retrieve her car, so she asked if they would drop them off at a restaurant before they left. The reporters obliged, and the three jumped out of the van, thanking them for the ride and dashing out of the rain into a packed restaurant.

Evangeline was exhausted and began crying when she saw a long line just to get a table or even a seat at the bar. The din of the crowded restaurant evaporated as the nine-year-old cried out, "I want my Mommy!"

The owner of the restaurant, recognizing their dire situation, set up cots in a small staff room in the back. It had a television so they could watch breaking news, and he brought them some sandwiches, chips, and cans of soda pop. Abequa thanked the owner for his generosity, and she and Wenonah devoured the fare. But Evangeline was neither hungry nor interested in sleeping. Her eyes glued to the television screen, she watched for any news of the rescue efforts.

As nightfall approached, Evangeline's eyes widened as she read a news bulletin banner that ran across the lower portion of the television screen:

THE U.S. COAST GUARD ANNOUNCES SUSPENSION OF RESCUE EFFORTS NEAR WHITEFISH POINT UNTIL MORNING. LOCAL AND STATE RESCUE EFFORTS ARE ALSO SUSPENDED BECAUSE OF POOR VISIBILITY AND DETERIORATING WEATHER CONDITIONS. STAY TUNED TO THIS STATION FOR UPDATES.

"Auntie, what do they mean by suspended?" Evangeline asked. "They aren't giving up, are they?"

"No, no, no," her aunt replied. "It just means they want to wait until they can see better. Your parents may already be on shore somewhere else, but they need to wait until daylight to find them. Now, let's get some rest, so we can get our car tomorrow and go back to the Point."

Evangeline laid down on the cot after her aunt turned off the television. She slept fitfully, tossing and turning.

The weather further deteriorated the next morning, and the National Weather Service issued an expanded gale warning for the entire shore of Lake Superior, from Marquette to Sault Ste. Marie. Waves as high as fourteen feet were being reported, and the Coast Guard announced all rescue efforts were called off.

Evangeline, now sitting up on her cot, listened as a reporter interviewed the captain of the U.S. Coast Guard on the local television station. The reporter asked about the prospects of finding survivors from the capsized vessels. The captain replied that the rescue mission was now re-classified as a recovery mission, as the missing flotilla members were not among the survivors found on the beach and could not have survived the turbulent, bone-chilling waters of Lake Superior.

"We presume they are lost," the captain concluded.

"Lost?" Evangeline cried out. "Why can't they find them?"

Abequa now faced the staggering reality that neither her husband nor her brother- and sister-in-law were ever coming back. Overwhelmed by her loss, she fell to her knees in shock and instinctively recited an Ojibwe prayer seeking intervention by the Great Spirit, with tears streaming down her cheeks.

"Auntie!" Evangeline repeated. "Why can't they find them?"

Summoning all of her courage, she struggled to her feet and turned to her grief-stricken nieces. She knew her conversation with the older niece was going to be hard enough, but it was going to be even more difficult to explain to young Evangeline.

After a brief and emotional conversation with Wenonah, the two embraced each other before composing themselves and turning towards

Evangeline, who was now paralyzed with fear. She saw the looks on the faces of her sister and aunt and put her hands over her ears as her aunt spoke.

"I can't hear you," she cried, as her aunt gently tried to deliver the bad news. Evangeline could feel her heart pumping so hard she thought it would burst, and she curled up in a ball on her cot for relief. Abequa and Wenonah attempted unsuccessfully to comfort the little girl, as the shock of losing both her parents had left her numb and oblivious to their words.

Nothing could be said or done to release Evangeline's pain. She remained outwardly silent but inwardly punished herself for not waving to them before they launched their fatal journey into Gitche Gumee.

With Evangeline's parents and uncle now presumed dead, Abequa packed up their meager belongings at the restaurant and together they walked to the nearby gas station to pick up the car. The owner, learning of their loss, waived the tow charges and filled up their gas tank.

"It's the least I can do, and I am so sorry for your loss," he told Abequa.

Overcome by emotion and so grateful for some generosity, she hugged him, a physical demonstration quite unusual for this otherwise stoic woman. They then drove to Abequa's house in the tiny town of Christmas, with the radio tuned to the news channel for any updates on the flotilla.

There would be no more news about the flotilla, and no bodies were recovered. Gitche Gumee had claimed its latest victims and taken them to its icy mansion below.

Stories about the Whitefish Point drownings filled the airwaves, and public outcries led the Canadian government to quietly and without fanfare announce that a pending application by a foreign transport company for a large-scale withdrawal of water from Lake Superior had been denied.

* * *

Upon their return to Christmas, tribal members traveled from far and wide to comfort Abequa in her time of need. They inquired about plans for a memorial service. It was too difficult to make such a decision so soon, especially since no bodies had been recovered. She did not respond immediately.

Abequa cut a long braid of her hair, as was custom when losing a spouse, and spent the next several days in prayers and meditation. Then, she announced her plans for a memorial service for her lost family members but decided that it would not be until Spring to avoid the uncertainties of a Michigan winter.

And it was a long, bitter winter for the LeBlanc sisters. The natural white beauty surrounding their Upper Peninsula house perched along the shore of Lake Superior could not overcome the lonely feeling of a home without parents.

After waiting a week for the pain to subside, Abequa attempted to ease their quiet suffering by encouraging the sisters to read the works of Henry Wadsworth Longfellow, whom their parents so loved. She gave them daily reading assignments and often recited aloud his poems and quotations before bedtime to give them something pleasant to dream about.

In time, Evangeline embraced Longfellow's stories and verse, but the older Wenonah, not so much.

Instead, Wenonah preferred to spend her free time following the political news in Washington and Lansing reported on radio and television networks, as well as talking with Frank about tribal issues.

Evangeline enjoyed learning about her heritage through Abequa's tales of the Ojibwe. Abequa encouraged her to use her exceptional voice to express those tales in song. The long winter days passed more agreeably as Evangeline sang aloud daily, much to the delight of her aunt.

After winter loosened its grip on the lakeshore and the day of the memorial service approached, Abequa arranged for the memorial ceremony to be held on a local ferry docked near the Pictured Rocks National Lakeshore, not far from the flotilla launch site. To lighten the somber mood and distract Evangeline from dwelling on the loss of her parents, Abequa asked Evangeline to sing at the service.

Evangeline's first song followed Wenonah's stirring tribute to their parents and a long organ interlude. Tears rolled down her cheeks as she sang a musical rendition of a Longfellow poem. After an emotional religious sermon, Evangeline closed the service by singing a favorite song of the North: Gordon Lightfoot's ballad, "The Wreck of the Edmund Fitzgerald."

As Evangeline sang the haunting words about Gitche Gumee never giving up its dead, she paused in the middle of the song, as thoughts of her lost parents lying beneath its waves raced through her mind. She fell to her knees and wept, with Wenonah rushing to her side to console her.

The audience, almost on cue, jumped to their feet. Joining hands, they sang the last words of the familiar ballad, with Evangeline and Wenonah clinging to each other and watching the audience sing and sway.

"It's magical," Wenonah whispered in her sister's ear. "Mother and Father are here with us today."

Evangeline felt the warmth of their presence, believing for the first time that her parents had not left her, but were merely spiritually transformed. I'm not alone anymore, she assured herself.

After the service, Abequa bought memorial headstones for her husband and her nieces' parents. The headstones were mounted at the old Mission Hill Cemetery, a historic First American resting place west of Sault Ste. Marie overlooking Canada.

It was not long after the memorial service that Wenonah announced her decision to leave Christmas and move to Sault Ste. Marie. She would work for her cousin Frank in the public relations office of the Kewadin tribal casino. Wenonah's passion for engaging in Native American politics would lead her to the state capitol in Lansing and eventually to Washington.

But Evangeline, now ten years old, stayed in Christmas and spent her early adulthood years under the protective watch of her widowed aunt. Growing up in a small house nestled along the lonely shores of Gitche Gumee, Evangeline's love of the Big Lake and First American traditions became her guiding passions.

She often walked to the nearby beach and stared at Gitche Gumee, determined to protect the great sea in whose arms her parents now rested.

Her mournful singing voice eventually became the vehicle through which she expressed her deepest emotions, first at church services and later at environmental rallies.

Until one day another force entered her life.

CHAPTER TWO

The Courtship

*"It is difficult to know at what moment love begins; it
is less difficult to know that it has begun."*

—Henry Wadsworth Longfellow

**ST. IGNACE, MICHIGAN
MAY 2020 (13 YEARS LATER)**

Now twenty-three years old, Evangeline was a popular head-
liner at Upper Peninsula environmental rallies. The tall, lithe young woman
with an olive complexion and raven black hair wore with pride her green
beaded headband and trademark, colorful wraparound skirts.

Many felt her songs uniquely captured the spirit of the environmental movement.

"I feel the spirits of my parents when I sing," she once told a reporter.
"It is for them I sing and for my beloved Gitche Gumee."

But while Evangeline was a local celebrity, she had read many glowing stories about another popular First American from downstate Michigan by the name of Joe Johnson. So many stories that she felt she knew him before ever meeting him.

Staring at the Mackinac Bridge straddling Lakes Huron and Michigan, she was both curious and anxious about news of his impending arrival at the St. Ignace rally where she was about to sing.

While sitting on a makeshift rally stage, stroking her hair and adjusting her headband, her concentration was broken by loud cries from the crowd. A black Ford F150 pulled up near the beach, and out of the cab jumped a large man she knew at once had to be him.

Evangeline saw the excitement he generated as he plunged through the crowd and bounded up to the stage where she was sitting.

He seemed even taller than she had imagined. With long black braided hair and broad shoulders, he carried his powerful frame with the energy and appearance of a much younger man, though she knew he had to be almost forty.

"Boozhoo!" he shouted in a loud booming voice as he mounted the stage, much to the delight of the First Americans in the crowd.

When a small group of hecklers shouted racial obscenities at him, his broad smile melted into a scowl that momentarily silenced both the hecklers and the crowd. Evangeline saw firsthand his ability to command respect.

When Frank, the organizer of this Line 5 protest, stepped to the microphone, the crowd was still mumbling about Joe. Her cousin was now the chief spokesperson for the Sault Tribe of Chippewa Indians and its Kewadin Casino in Sault Ste Marie. Dubbed "the Soo" by the locals, the economy of this aging northern Michigan town was heavily dependent upon the tourist dollars generated by its two principal attractions: the Soo Locks and the Kewadin casino he represented.

"Shut it down!" Frank yelled, pumping his fist in the air and pointing to the lake where an underwater oil pipeline known as Line 5 rested.

Whistles and car horns filled the air in response.

"The Great Spirit will punish those who desecrate our freshwater seas, and we as his children must smote those who defile it with the black death they call oil."

The crowd roared their approval, chanting, "Shut it down, shut it down, shut it down!"

After allowing the chants to continue for several minutes, Frank raised both of his arms for silence.

He announced Evangeline would open the rally with a song she created just for the rally, followed by a speech from their special guest.

The crowd again howled their approval as Evangeline approached the microphone. She felt uneasy as the eyes of the featured speaker followed her. She was so nervous that she forgot the opening words of her song, pausing and blushing in embarrassment as her guitar accompanist had to repeat the opening line of the melody.

But the crowd urged her on.

She glanced back at Joe Johnson, who was smiling and waving for her to continue.

Composing herself, Evangeline found her voice and held the crowd in awe, as her mournful song about the struggle against the pipeline brought both cheers and tears to all within earshot.

She finished the last lines of her song, played to the melody of the song "Amazing Grace," with a call to action:

Let us not rest until we see

The waters clear and blue,

Then we will know our lake is free,

Protect our shining sea

When she finished her song, there was a momentary hush as the crowd absorbed her words. Then, spontaneously, the crowd broke out in cheers.

She beamed with pride at the crowd's reaction but was startled when a pair of large hands pressed on her shoulders, as Joe shouted praises of her performance and egged the crowd on.

Both exhilarated and somewhat embarrassed by Joe's lauds, she retreated from the microphone, yielding him center stage.

He walked to the edge of the stage. With one arm thrust in the air, he pushed away the microphone and shouted out in a loud voice: "Can you hear me?"

The crowd shouted its loud approval in response.

"I said, can you HEAR ME?" he repeated.

A thunderous crowd response followed, lasting nearly a minute, with car horns and whistles adding to the din.

"Well," he continued, "that was one hell of a performance. What a tough act to follow!" he shouted, pointing to Evangeline.

"How can we lose when we have a voice like that on our side? She has the power of the Great Spirit in her."

The crowd responded with a "Velvet, Velvet" chant, a popular name the crowd used to show their love of her voice.

Evangeline noticed Joe's startled look at the spontaneity of the crowd's response out of the corner of her eye. He turned towards her and nodded with a broad but puzzled smile.

Then Joe turned to the heart of his speech; a rallying cry against Line 5.

He reminded the crowd of the many treaties broken by the greed of whites, a familiar story that Abequa had shared with Evangeline years ago. The crowd shouted in agreement with each major transgression he excoriated.

"And now their greed for oil is threatening to pollute our great fresh-water seas! It must stop now!" he shouted, with the crowd chanting their approval and car horns blaring.

Evangeline was now engulfed in the moment. Not since her parents' radio interview had she felt such pride being a First American. She jumped to her feet in approval.

After several minutes of blasting the nearby underwater pipeline and the threat it posed to the Great Lakes, he finished his speech with a poetic clarion call:

For we First Americans and for those who followed us,

Mother Earth is neither Republican nor Democrat.

She is not a commodity to be bought or sold.

She represents who we are and what we value in life.

It is our sacred trust to protect her against all enemies,

be they tormentors or appeasers.

So, let us go forth united and pledge our eternal vigilance to protect her

as we would protect our children.

The Great Spirit, our ancestors, our children, and our children's children expect no less

Join hands in harmony with Mother Earth

And unsheathe our weapons of righteousness to defend her with our very lives.

Death we fear not in defense of our Mother.

Evangeline again leapt to her feet in excitement. He had unleashed the same passion she had seen in her parents at environmental rallies over a decade ago.

Joe then plunged into the welcoming crowd, and Evangeline stepped off the stage to join her aunt.

Two cameramen approached her and asked if she would pose for pictures, as she was striking in her colorful native clothing.

She readily agreed and walked back up to the podium to pose.

While she was being photographed, Frank told Abequa that Joe was going to nearby Mackinac Island the next day to view the damage caused by the Line 5 pipeline oil spill earlier that year. He had asked if Evangeline would join them there.

"We can't stay here overnight. We need to drive back to Christmas, as I have some errands to run and a doctor's appointment," Abequa snorted.

"Don't worry. She can stay at my house in the Soo today and I'll bring her back to the ferry dock tomorrow morning. After the island tour, I'll drive her back to Christmas," he responded.

Abequa was still uneasy about the invitation.

Since the death of Evangeline's parents, Abequa had tried to shield her niece from the painful memories of their death and the racial ugliness that constantly followed Evangeline's parents during their many protest rallies.

She felt that same ugliness at this rally when she heard the hateful chants from hecklers when Joe first arrived and saw a sign that read "No More Johnson, More Singing Squaw." And she worried about Joe's intentions towards her young niece.

"It's irresponsible to let Evangeline consort with a politician she only just met," she told Frank.

But Frank was insistent, arguing that it was an important introduction for Evangeline. Joe Johnson was a key player in the environmental movement, and Evangeline could learn a great deal from him about the broader national environmental agenda. He assured Abequa that he would be with her during the entire tour, so she would never be alone.

Abequa still resisted, but when the photo session finished and Evangeline rejoined them, Frank blurted out Joe's invitation to Mackinac Island, much to the consternation of Abequa.

Evangeline's eyes lit up with excitement. A trip to the island with a legend! But from the look in her aunt's eyes, Evangeline could see Abequa did not share her sentiment.

"Oh, Auntie, please understand. This is a dream come true. A trip to the island with Joe Johnson. This means so much in our battle to shut down Line 5."

After several minutes of continued pleading, Abequa finally nodded her approval with one caveat.

"There will be no horseplay," she warned.

"Don't worry, Auntie," Evangeline laughed. "This is about protecting Gitche Gumee and nothing more."

Her ride to the Soo was a nonstop conversation, as Evangeline peppered Frank with questions about Joe. By the time she arrived at Frank's house, his answers had only heightened her expectations of the trip.

She closed her eyes, dreaming about how the next day might unfold.

* * *

It was about an hour's drive from the Soo back to St. Ignace. Evangeline had picked out her favorite wraparound dress to wear for the island trek. When they arrived at the ferry dock the next morning, she spotted Joe and a young man standing close beside him whom she did not recognize, surrounded by a group of local reporters and cameramen.

When Joe saw Evangeline and Frank pull up, he excused himself, and he and the young man briskly walked to her car.

"I was talking to Frank about you yesterday, and I am so glad you're coming with us," he said, extending his hand to help her out of the car. "He told me your aunt was not a big fan of this trip and that she was well named," he chuckled, referring to the Chippewa origin of Abequa's name, which means "She stays home."

"And your name, Evangeline, as in the Longfellow poem?"

It impressed her he knew the literary origin of her name. Her parents were such huge fans of Longfellow that they named their children after Longfellow characters.

"But I heard the crowd call you Velvet," he said with a puzzled face.

"Yes, that's right. Many find my name too formal, so they just call me Velvet," she acknowledged.

"What a perfect name. Do you mind if I call you Velvet?" he asked.

"Oh, please do."

"Call me Joe, and this is my driver, Taylor Grant. Really, he is more than just a driver; but I'm reckless on the road, so he has kept me alive for the last couple of years. He's a CMU grad."

"CMU?" she asked.

"Central Michigan University. He played football there. Yes, he and I are both trolls from below the bridge. I hope you Yoopers can forgive our invasion of your beautiful U.P."

Velvet was struck by the contrast between the blonde hair, blue-eyed Taylor and his towering, black-haired First American boss. While Joe was an intriguing celebrity, she also was attracted to this handsome, athletically built young man with an engaging smile.

After exchanging pleasantries and extolling the beauty of the nearby lake, Frank encouraged them to board the ferry. The horn had already blown, signaling its imminent departure.

Following a short ferry ride to the island, a horse-drawn carriage was waiting at the island dock to take them to the western shore, site of the earlier oil spill. Since Mackinac Island is a rare state park where private motor vehicles are not permitted, it was a slow ride to the site, but it gave Joe and Evangeline time to become better acquainted.

The two-bench, four-passenger carriage created an awkward situation: who would sit next to Joe? As he was a large man, it fell to the slightest of them to join him, and Evangeline gingerly slid onto the bench. Joe smiled at her, and their hands touched ever so gently. Feelings of warmth towards this friendly man soon overcame the awkwardness of the moment.

"You know, I heard stories about a First American woman singing at protest rallies up north while I was downstate in Mount Pleasant, but I didn't know you were the source of those songs. And by the way, the news accounts didn't do your voice justice. Your song was incredible."

It surprised Evangeline that news of her songs reached that far south, but she was far more interested in knowing more about him, so she turned the conversation to his background.

Joe regaled her with stories about tribal issues in the Lower Peninsula of Michigan. First American problems in Mount Pleasant seemed eerily similar to those Evangeline had experienced in the Upper Peninsula. He's a real fighter who could do something about them, she mused as the carriage ride proceeded.

When the carriage arrived at the western-most edge of the island, Evangeline detected a faint scent of petroleum, and the water near the shore had a darker sheen than the rest of the blue Lake Huron water farther from the shore. When the four stepped off the carriage, she noticed a change in Joe's demeanor. She was not sure whether it was anger or a sadness, but the friendly conversation in the carriage ended as he stared silently at the beach and the tainted water.

Taylor and Frank stayed by the carriage while Joe and Evangeline walked over the rocks to the sandy beach. Frank shouted a warning that the rocks between the carriage path and the beach might be slippery from the oil.

Almost on cue, Velvet slipped on the rocks, but Joe caught her, embracing her in his brawny arms. Their eyes locked for just a few seconds before he released her. Then they proceeded together towards the water, Evangeline experiencing a powerful emotional moment in their brief, intimate encounter.

When she reached the sandy beach, Velvet spotted a small puddle of water covered with a thin layer of petroleum. In the puddle, she also saw a faint movement, as a creature was trying to escape its oily prison. She bent down and scooped up the tiny creature which, after wiping off the oil, she recognized as a leopard frog.

The frog was barely moving. Seeking release from the black death coating had sapped most of its strength.

Joe leaned down beside her and looked at the struggling creature.

"I'm afraid he's a goner," he pronounced.

Evangeline looked at Joe and saw in his face the same sadness she was feeling. Then she looked down at the poor creature in her hands as it stopped moving altogether. Tears rolled down her face as she began chanting an Ojibwe prayer to the now lifeless creature in her hand.

When she finished the prayer, she noticed a strange expression on Joe's face. Did he think she was foolish singing to a frog, she wondered?

She stood up, kicking off her shoes, and walked towards a shallow part of the water that was less tainted and released the creature. Waves bobbed its body up and down, dragging the frog away from the beach and into the deeper water. Evangeline watched as the small body slowly disappeared below the surface.

As she turned her gaze away from the lake, Joe was standing right behind her. Instinctively, she reached out to him for comfort, flinging her arms around his waist and resting her head on his chest. A feeling of warmth and safety enveloped her.

Recognizing her actions could be misinterpreted, she apologized for her emotional outburst and gently pushed away from him. But Joe just smiled.

"That was a beautiful moment," he replied softly.

When they returned to the carriage, Frank noted her wet skirt and asked why she had waded into the lake. Evangeline described the death of the frog as a tragic lingering effect of the oil spill from the Line 5 pipeline break.

"Why is nothing being done to stop the fouling of our water?" she exclaimed.

Taylor responded, describing how CMU student environmental organizations were lobbying the state legislature to shut down the pipeline. He also praised Joe for his tireless work with the state legislature to push the anti-pipeline legislation.

Evangeline looked at Joe for an explanation.

"Velvet, I have been working state legislators on both sides of the aisle to get this legislation passed, but with little success. The Republicans have stymied our efforts. We have a better chance getting legislation passed in Congress, but your congressman has made legislating difficult there as well," Joe explained.

"Doesn't he see the danger of this underwater pipeline?" she asked.

"It's about campaign contributions and the need for propane gas in the Upper Peninsula," Frank interjected.

"His Democratic challenger has pledged to introduce legislation to shut down the pipeline, but he's a long shot to win," Taylor added.

"So, what can we do to help?" Evangeline asked.

"Well, we have to campaign like hell for him," Joe responded.

"Tell me how," Evangeline replied.

The four spent the rest of the carriage ride brainstorming a strategy to defeat the incumbent. Evangeline marveled as the three men outlined a plan to campaign throughout the sprawling First Congressional District, describing a political world so foreign to her parochial upbringing.

Joe and Taylor pledged to make more campaign trips to the Upper Peninsula and Northern Lower Peninsula counties of the district to help the candidate. Frank reminded them of the many tribally owned casinos in the district, promising to rally tribal voters and pledging increased tribal financial support for the Democratic challenger.

"What can I do?" Evangeline asked.

Joe looked at her earnestly and said, "You can use that beautiful voice of yours and sing at his campaign rallies. He has had trouble getting media coverage, so your singing at his events would be an enormous boost," Joe asserted.

Evangeline paused, recognizing she would be entering a realm that her aunt had warned her to avoid. To sing at environmental rallies was one thing. To sing at a political campaign rally was something else.

"I'll think about it, but I want to talk with my aunt and my sister, Wenonah."

"Wenonah? Your sister isn't Wenonah LeBlanc, is she?" Joe asked.

"Yes, do you know her?" she responded.

"I only know one person named Wenonah LeBlanc, and she is one of the most influential Native American lobbyists in D.C. How foolish of me not to connect the LeBlanc name. I didn't know you had such strong political ties," Joe exclaimed.

"My sister is the political animal in the family, not me," she added.

Evangeline noticed the smiling nod of approval Joe gave Taylor, wondering what that nod meant, but continued to listen with great interest to the campaign mechanics.

The ferry ride back to St. Ignace was a lively one, as the four mapped out their new political journey. While Evangeline was intrigued by their campaign strategy, she was still uncertain whether she was ready to enter the political world.

When the ferry docked in St. Ignace, Joe asked again if she would seriously consider a singing commitment for the 2020 Congressional campaign. She nodded she would, and he gave her a farewell hug that was unexpected but not unwelcome.

"I'll be calling you soon," he promised.

On her car ride back to Christmas, Frank explained the mechanics of her getting involved in the 2020 Congressional race.

"I know little about political campaigns. It sounds challenging, but in a way exciting as well," Evangeline said.

"You will learn much from Joe," Frank replied.

But even more important than her concerns about her political inexperience were the personal questions she had about Joe. She pressed Frank about whether Joe was married. Was there anything about him that should concern her? Was he honest? Was he the real deal?

Frank demurred and said those were questions better posed to Wenonah. He added that she also needed to talk with Abequa, who would be a strong opponent of such a move.

On their trip back to Mount Pleasant, Joe quizzed Taylor about Evangeline LeBlanc. What did Taylor know about her beyond her singing efforts and her sister Wenonah?

Anticipating Joe's interest in Evangeline, Taylor had texted student leaders at CMU.

"I learned she has lived with her aunt in the little village of Christmas ever since her parents drowned during a kayak protest movement over a decade ago."

"The Whitefish Point flotilla drownings?"

"I believe so," Taylor responded.

"You mean Art and Margaret LeBlanc were her *parents?*" Joe exclaimed.

"Yes, I think those were their names, but I'll have to double check on it," Taylor nodded. "And she lost her uncle, too."

Now Evangeline thoroughly intrigued Joe. A beautiful woman with a haunting voice linked to a beloved Sault tribal couple and a politically well-connected sister. What a dynamite combination!

"I really feel foolish for not making those connections. Taylor, find everything you can about Evangeline LeBlanc."

"Is this a political or personal request?" Taylor asked.

"Both," he replied.

What an incredible woman, he thought. And what a great political asset!

Joe paused and added one more request. "And Taylor, get me her personal cell phone number. I have some bridges to build."

CHAPTER THREE

Guess Who's Coming to Dinner?

"Politics doesn't make strange bedfellows—marriage does."

—Groucho Marx

CHRISTMAS, MICHIGAN
AUGUST 2020

OVER THE NEXT TWO MONTHS, EVANGELINE RECEIVED ALMOST DAILY calls from Joe. After Evangeline's constant pleading, Abequa dropped her objection to Evangeline joining the 2020 campaign, but only after Evangeline promised limited involvement and regular contact with Wenonah.

Almost nightly, she called Wenonah in Washington to learn more about the congressional campaign, but their conversations inevitably gravitated towards Joe's personal life.

Then there were the political questions. Did he really care about First American issues, or was this just a front? Were there any rumors or scandals surrounding him she should know about?

"I don't know of any scandals or political dirt on Joe, but only you can judge his character," Wenonah counseled. "You have always been a quick study of people. Why don't you invite him to dinner and judge for yourself?"

Evangeline was silent as she pondered this next step. Am I ready for this, she thought to herself?

"But what about Auntie? Won't she …?"

"I will fly out to be there with you," Wenonah volunteered. "And you know Auntie. She can smell a phony a mile away," Wenonah laughed. "Between the two of us, we will find answers to your questions about Joe."

"Let me talk to Auntie about dinner. If I can convince her, I'll give it a shot," Evangeline promised.

While Abequa was not happy about the idea, she reluctantly agreed, and Evangeline invited Joe to dinner in early August.

He immediately accepted.

But the day before his arrival, Evangeline had second thoughts about the invitation. What if Abequa didn't like him? What then? It was a gamble, for sure. But she sensed it was time to take the next step in their relationship.

When he arrived, Evangeline immediately sensed the tension between Abequa and Joe. While Joe outwardly was all smiles and enthusiasm, Abequa sat silently in her rocking chair, her eyes glued to a snowy television screen. She acknowledged his presence only when he commented on Abequa's cozy house.

Wenonah tried to break the tension by asking playfully what he thought people might say about him consorting with a woman named Velvet?

"From the moment I heard her sing in St. Ignace and the crowd's response calling her Velvet, I thought the name captured who she truly was—a beautiful woman with a voice as soft as velvet."

"Her name is Evangeline," Abequa interrupted. "Her deceased parents gave her that name because of their love of Longfellow poetry, and we don't need some downstate troll to change that."

"I meant no disrespect," Joe responded.

"Oh Auntie," Wenonah jumped in, "you've been living alone too long to recognize a lovely compliment when you hear one."

Evangeline saw her chance to chime in.

"I like the name Velvet. I don't think it disrespects Mother and Father. I am more than just the daughter of my parents. I have my own voice and my own vision."

Joe and Wenonah nodded in agreement, but Abequa just frowned.

"Well Auntie," Evangeline continued, "I want those who love me—family and friends—to call me Velvet. If you or others do not, that's OK too."

After an uncomfortable pause in the conversation, Wenonah rose and announced that dinner was getting cold. Abequa nodded, rose, and walked to the head of the table, ensuring that no one would sit on either side of her.

The dinner conversation was much less confrontational, with Joe displaying an impressive grasp of First American policy issues and a willingness to entertain a wide range of personal questions. The only serious disagreement that arose was how Evangeline was to be addressed. Wenonah and Joe referred to her as "Velvet" throughout dinner.

But Abequa was strident in her reference to her niece.

"*Evangeline,* pass the salt please," she would say loudly after Joe or Wenonah addressed her as Velvet.

After dinner and an exchange of pleasantries, Abequa announced it was getting late, and she was going to bed.

"Good night, Mr. Johnson," she announced, looking at both him and the front door.

Joe took the hint and texted Taylor for a ride to a motel in nearby Munising.

"Joe?" Evangeline interjected but also glancing at her aunt for a reaction. "Would you like to stay here for the night? We can put you up on the sofa."

Velvet saw the fury in her aunt's eyes at the suggestion, but Joe gracefully declined.

"Velvet, that's very kind, but your aunt is right. It's late and I already have hotel reservations. But I'll take a raincheck!"

Velvet saw the harshness of her aunt's face soften at Joe's deference to her obvious wishes. That's a good sign, she thought.

After Joe left, Velvet turned to her family for their reactions.

"Well, what do you think of him now?" she asked.

"I guess you could do worse; he could be a WHITE politician," Abequa replied, waving her hand dismissively and then walking to her bedroom.

Wenonah laughed aloud at the back-handed compliment.

"That's as close to a passing grade as you're ever going to get from her."

Velvet smiled in agreement but pressed Wenonah for her reaction to Joe as a person.

"Wenonah, is he for real or just another ambitious politician?"

"He seems real to me from our conversation tonight," Wenonah replied. "I never worked directly with him before, but my staff say that his concern for First American issues and the environment is genuine."

"But do you like him?" Evangeline continued.

"Well, VELVET," Wenonah responded, "enough that I'm going to call you Velvet from now on."

Velvet realized that the two most important people in her life had given Joe a passing grade.

Could he be the one, she thought?

* * *

In the weeks that followed, Velvet eagerly looked forward to Joe's calls. When he suggested they appear together on stage with the Democratic challenger at the 2020 Labor Day rally in nearby Munising, she readily agreed.

The crowd at the rally was rocking, and Joe and Velvet joined hands with their candidate at the end to the rousing approval of the crowd.

"This is so exciting," Velvet exclaimed to Joe over the din of the crowd.

But she saw tension in the candidate's face, and it was not one of excitement. The candidate did not thank Joe and Velvet, but rushed to his car, phone in hand.

Strange, thought Velvet. Something must be up. But the rally was still a high point in the campaign, and everyone seemed upbeat.

As they stepped off the makeshift campaign stage, Taylor took Joe and Velvet aside and delivered some devastating political news. Their candidate was accused of having an extramarital affair with one of his married campaign staff members and was considering dropping out of the race. With only two months before the general election, his departure would ensure the incumbent's reelection.

Velvet watched as Joe grabbed his phone and called the candidate's campaign manager. She saw his face drop as the conversation continued, knowing that bad news was coming.

After ending his telephone conversation, he turned and said the words no supporter would ever want to hear: "Well, it'll be official tomorrow morning, but our candidate is dropping out of the race," Joe recounted, avoiding all eye contact.

"What does that mean? Can we get someone else to take his place?" Velvet asked.

"Who would want to enter the race with only two months left to campaign?" Joe responded.

"After all of our work, we can't give up without a fight," Velvet protested. "Can anyone take his place? Joe, could you run?"

She saw a strange look on the faces of both Taylor and Joe, and an awkward silence ensued before Taylor responded.

"Not unless he lived in the First District, which he currently does not," Taylor responded.

Taylor's use of the word "currently" seemed curious to Velvet, but she continued to ask what they still could do before the November general election.

She reached for her cell phone and called Wenonah for advice, though she had a sinking feeling that the campaign was doomed.

Wenonah confirmed her assumption. The 2020 First Congressional District Democratic campaign was dead.

Joe was furious about the revelation.

"How could he be so stupid?" Joe muttered. "And with a staff member?" he shouted indignantly. "Whatever happened to staff loyalty?"

Velvet was too shaken to think deeply about why Joe would frame the problem as one of staff disloyalty rather than the candidate's personal infidelity. It crushed her that her first campaign experience would abruptly end on such a disastrous note.

Joe and Velvet stared at each other in silence for several moments.

"Campaign Lesson 101: Expect the unexpected," Joe responded in resignation to Velvet's quizzical look.

Then Taylor warned they should leave before the press found them and asked some tough questions.

After a few brief words of reflection on the campaign, Joe and Taylor left for Mount Pleasant, and Velvet left with Frank to her home to Christmas.

They agreed to stay in touch.

* * *

Shortly after her return to Christmas, Abequa's health deteriorated rapidly, and Velvet's focus turned exclusively to her ailing aunt. Reluctantly, Joe made less frequent calls to Evangeline and only one brief visit to

Christmas in the weeks prior to the 2020 November election in deference to her wishes.

Sometimes Joe's calls went unanswered for several days, but Velvet felt duty bound to care for her aunt. Joe respected her need for space.

The 2020 November election outcome was a foregone conclusion, as the Republican incumbent won 75 percent of the vote. Joe had predicted many Democrats would cross over to the Green Party when the Democratic candidate withdrew, and there were indeed a surprising number of voters who did so.

But Velvet was too concerned about her aunt's health to talk about politics. Instead, she stayed by her ailing aunt's side, as Abequa was experiencing worrisome, short-term memory loss.

With the Christmas holiday fast approaching, Abequa lapsed into a semi-comatose state. Velvet knew the end was near, but she hoped Abequa would live at least through Christmas day. I want Christmas Day to be remembered as a day of birth, not death, she prayed.

However, Abequa had difficulty breathing, so Velvet had her transferred to a hospice facility in Munising on Christmas Eve. Velvet broke into tears as the hospice director told her that her aunt would likely not last another night. She called Wenonah to deliver the bad news, and both cried as they absorbed the magnitude of her passing.

She stayed by her aunt's bedside throughout the night, holding her aunt's hand and singing some of her aunt's favorite Ojibwe songs. Abequa's breathing became more and more labored and then, at the stroke of noon on Christmas Day, she was no more.

"Oh Auntie, don't leave me," she cried out as she kissed her aunt on the forehead.

An attendant heard the cry and entered the room, but Velvet waved her away and asked for time alone to say goodbye. She then laid on the bed beside her deceased aunt and sobbed.

When the attendant later returned to the room, Evangeline rose, red-eyed from crying, and walked to the window. She looked at a world which would no longer feel the footsteps of her aunt.

I will have her buried near the headstones of my uncle and my parents in the old Mission Hill Cemetery, she decided. The spirits of all my family will be together again, she told herself, and old Mission Hill Cemetery will become my new spiritual home.

Abequa's memorial service was held on New Year's Eve in Munising. Because of the holiday season and winter weather, the service was sparsely attended. However, both Joe and Taylor came, and Velvet hugged them warmly. They had respected her wishes to be alone with her aunt, but now they were there to comfort her.

No longer restrained by her aunt's resistance to Joe and faced with the reality of living alone in her aunt's home in isolated Christmas, Velvet thought of Joe differently, as someone who could fill the void of her aunt's passing and offer security at this insecure moment of her life.

Joe and Taylor joined Frank and Wenonah for lunch following the service, and the conversation revolved around Velvet, who talked at length about growing up with her aunt. This was the first time she had talked about her early years with anyone other than Wenonah, and it felt good to unburden herself with friends and family.

She had lived a sheltered life, she admitted. She was home schooled, with limited travel and few close personal friends outside the village. "But," she added, "my life has not been without its moments of artistic and spiritual inspiration thanks to Auntie. I would never have sung at rallies without the help of Auntie's stories of our culture and the readings of Longfellow," she confessed. "However, I know little about life below the Mackinac Bridge and the political world that this campaign unveiled."

Velvet paused, looking at Wenonah. "I probably don't belong in the world of politics like Wenonah," she confessed.

Wenonah jumped in.

"You belong there as much as any woman. You have such great personal instincts and care so passionately for our people and our land," Wenonah interjected.

Velvet blushed, but abruptly changed the subject.

"Enough about me. What about you guys?"

The luncheon conversation turned to Taylor and Joe, and what had been happening in their lives since the collapse of the 2020 Congressional campaign.

Taylor had graduated from CMU in December with a degree in interpersonal communications and would start graduate school there in early January. It impressed her he could juggle his studies while working for Joe and continuing his student environmental leadership activities.

She was attracted to Taylor's warm smile and his willingness to explain in understandable terms the complexities of the political world she had just entered. I wish I had known him when I was growing up in Christmas, she mused. Maybe I would have been more interested in politics like Wenonah.

Then the conversation turned to Joe.

Joe had been re-elected to the Saginaw Chippewa Tribal Council. The Mount Pleasant-based tribe operated the huge Soaring Eagle Casino and Resort, an important partner in the Mount Pleasant community. While he was deeply involved in mid-Michigan issues, he confessed he missed being up north fighting to shut down the Line 5 pipeline.

Velvet noticed the marked change in his tone when he mentioned Line 5. There was more emotional intensity in Joe's voice as he expressed fear of another Line 5 spill.

However, it was Wenonah who dropped the political bombshell of the day with her off-the-cuff comment. "Well, Joe, it looks like both you and Velvet will vote for the same congressional representative in 2022."

"What?" Velvet asked.

"Because of the 2020 census," Wenonah explained, "the boundaries of the First Congressional District of Michigan had to be expanded south because of a decline in population. It replaced the Second Congressional

District of Maine as the largest district east of the Mississippi River, stretching 500 miles from the tip of the Upper Peninsula to the center of the Lower Peninsula. By expanding farther south, the district added Isabella County and an important constituency—the Saginaw Chippewa Indian Tribe—at its southern-most boundary.

"So, the Michigan Democrats are looking at the First Congressional District as their best chance in 2022 to elect a new Democratic Member of Congress," Wenonah responded, looking directly at Joe.

Velvet saw Joe and Taylor glance at each other, but neither responded.

"Joe, are you thinking about running for Congress?" Velvet blurted out.

"Well, the thought has crossed my mind. It would take a lot of legwork and a lot of money to unseat the Republican incumbent."

Taylor piped in, "Joe has good name recognition and solid support in Mount Pleasant and mid-Michigan, but he could use some help in your neck of the woods, Velvet."

"I can help with that. I really can. Why don't you come to our rallies across the U.P.," she urged. "I know little about national politics, but I know how dreadful our congressman has been for First Americans and our environment."

Joe smiled at her but had a serious look in his eyes.

Velvet caught his change in mood. It seemed a Joe Johnson congressional campaign was more than just an idle thought.

Taylor opened his mouth to respond, but Joe waved his hand and looked directly at Velvet. "Velvet, if you will help me win over the hearts of voters in the U.P., I will seriously consider it," he countered.

Velvet was flattered that Joe would make her an important part of his decision, and equally excited about the prospect of working closely with him.

She glanced at Wenonah, who was now beaming.

"Joe Johnson, I will certainly consider your proposition," Velvet replied.

The conversation then switched to other pleasantries. When lunch ended, the parties departed Munising, each going their separate ways.

* * *

In the weeks following Abequa's memorial service, Joe's calls and visits became more frequent as he outlined his campaign plans and his need for her to join him.

On Valentine's Day, amidst a snowy Upper Peninsula evening, Velvet heard a knock on her door. Who on earth would visit me during a snowstorm, she wondered? When she opened the door, she gasped in astonishment.

"Happy Valentine's Day, Velvet," a snow-covered Joe whispered.

"Joe, what are you doing here in such a storm?" Velvet exclaimed, inviting him inside.

He smiled and handed her a bouquet of red roses, now coated with fluffy white snowflakes.

"I couldn't get the florist to bring you flowers on this special day, so I brought them myself."

"Did Taylor drive you here?" she asked.

"No, he had other plans for the day, so I left him in the Soo and drove here myself," Joe chuckled. "Didn't realize it was snowing this hard until I was more than halfway here."

"Well, come take off your snowy clothes and sit by the fire to warm up. I can't believe you would come all this way in this weather just to bring me flowers."

"Well, I had another reason for coming," he replied mysteriously.

There was a long pause, and Velvet stared at him, waiting for him to finish.

"Velvet, you are very special to me. More than special. I can't get you out of my mind. I want you more than I have ever wanted anyone in my life."

Velvet trembled as Joe reached in his pocket and pulled out a small box tied with a green ribbon, which he handed to her.

She had difficulty untying the ribbon, so he reached over and loosened the bow with a sharp tug. Inside the somewhat tattered box was a gold ring with a heart-shaped emerald surrounded by tiny diamonds.

"Velvet, my grandmother gave me this ring before she passed, and said to give it only to the one I truly love."

Velvet was speechless. He leaned towards her, and she hugged him.

"I don't know what to say, Joe. I am overwhelmed."

"Say you feel the same way as I do," he replied. "I want you to be with me always as I fight for our people and our land."

"This is all so sudden. You know I care for you very much."

"But?" he added.

"No buts, Joe. I just wasn't prepared for this."

"I understand. Maybe I should go now."

"It's storming outside. Are you sure it's safe?" she asked.

"Munising is not far, so I'll grab a room there tonight and give you some space."

"OK, if you're sure," Velvet replied.

"Yeah, I'll be fine," Joe said, pulling his coat back on as he headed to the door.

As he opened the door, Velvet gave him a kiss on the cheek.

Joe smiled, braving the cold as he headed towards his car.

I never had such feelings for a man before. I never even seriously thought about marriage before. Am I being too cautious, she asked herself as she watched Joe drive off? Is the wife of a politician my new destiny?

She spent the rest of the evening on the phone with Wenonah, describing her day.

"How would you have responded to Joe?" she asked Wenonah. "Would you have said yes right then?"

Velvet waited impatiently as Wenonah paused before responding.

Wenonah then replied with her own question, "Do you want to marry him?"

"I don't know. I really had not thought about marriage before."

"Well, sleep on it. You don't have to make such an important decision now," Wenonah replied. "It's a decision that will change your entire life, so take your time, sis."

Velvet agreed and bade her sister good night. How she wished her parents were there to talk about marriage. But the old Mission Hill Cemetery was snowbound, the bodies of her parents were in the arms of Gitche Gumee, and her aunt's body remained in a morgue awaiting the spring thaw.

She spent a restless night searching her soul for an answer, alone in her bed.

The next morning, as she opened her curtains to gaze at the fresh winter wonderland of snow, she saw a vehicle pulling up her snow-covered driveway.

Was it Joe?

The doorbell rang, and she rushed to the door, only to find a man with a package. She then saw the sign on the truck that read "Amazon."

Deflated, she took the package, thanking the driver for making the journey. When she opened the package, she found a heart-shaped quill box and a note from Joe that read:

Hoping to find a place in your heart.

Love Joe

In the days and weeks ahead, his calls came at noon, a special time of the day commemorating the loss of both her parents and her aunt.

She knew she loved him, but she also had to weigh whether she was ready to assume the role of a politician's wife. Abequa had told her most politicians were self-serving and dishonest. But Joe seemed to be the exception.

After the snow had sufficiently melted, she traveled to old Mission Hill Cemetery to share her decision with her parents. She knelt by their gravestones and brushed aside vines that partially covered the LeBlanc names, speaking aloud to them.

"Mother and Father, I miss you so. I want you to know that I have found a person I love and who can help me carry on your mission to protect our people and Gitche Gumee. Help me and guide me as I continue the journey you began so many years ago at Whitefish Point."

After the prayer, she arose and looked around the cemetery. She noticed a few long wooden spirit houses perched over some of the older graves. Abequa had taught her that spirit houses protected the body while the soul crossed over to the spirit world, with a round hole cut on the western end of the structure for the deceased's spirit to escape. Most had a small shelf by the opening to leave food offerings or other special gifts.

She stared at the temporary grave marker where her aunt's body would soon rest. I hope someone prepares a spirit house for her, she thought.

Lacking a spirit house shelf, she had no place to leave a remembrance for her aunt. "I miss you so much, Auntie, but I'm OK. Don't worry about me."

She wandered back to her car and drove to the Soo to talk with Frank about marrying Joe and the political campaign ahead.

"It'll be a whole new world for you, Velvet. It'll be very tough as a First American woman, but I know you and Joe together can move mountains," Frank counseled.

She stayed that night at the Soo casino hotel, dining with Frank and then retiring early, eager to get back to Christmas.

When she returned home the next day, she made herself a cup of hot green tea and then dialed Joe's telephone number.

When he answered the phone, she paused, weighing her next words.

"Joe, do you want to marry me? "

"Velvet, more than anything else in the world," he replied without hesitation.

"Then my answer is yes."

CHAPTER FOUR

The Long and Winding Road to Congress

"Whenever a man has cast a longing eye on offices,
a rottenness begins in his conduct"

—Thomas Jefferson

CHRISTMAS, MICHIGAN
MARCH 2021–DECEMBER 2023

A DIRTY WHITE CLAPBOARD CHURCH IN NEARBY MUNISING HOSTED their private wedding ceremony on March 15. At their request, only Wenonah, Frank, and a few of Joe's family and friends attended.

Before exchanging vows, Velvet decided to keep her family name but, as a gesture to Joe, she signed her wedding certificate "Velvet LeBlanc", adopting the nickname he and her followers had given her.

The couple spent their honeymoon in a cabin near Copper Harbor at the tip of the Keweenaw Peninsula, the northernmost part of the Upper Peninsula. The location was idyllic, marking the deepest penetration of land into the heart of Lake Superior. But the honeymoon bonding was less than ideal because of Velvet's shyness and sexual inexperience.

Joe cut their honeymoon short, and they returned to the business at hand: wresting control of the newly expanded First Congressional District from its incumbent congressman.

"It's all right, Velvet," Joe consoled her. "Our love will grow as we fight together to win this race."

Velvet prayed he was right.

Over the next 20 months, Joe and Velvet crisscrossed the sprawling district, passion for their cause often substituting for the deep personal intimacy their relationship lacked. The campaign was grueling and, at times, disheartening. Racial slurs and vandalism were not uncommon, but Joe assured her these were acts by cowards who posed no physical threat to him or her.

Velvet remembered warnings from Frank and Abequa about the ugliness of politics, but vowed to overcome the voices of ignorance and bigotry. Her parents withstood such attacks and so should she.

Velvet's involvement in the environmental movement earned her the support of thousands of college students and younger voters throughout the Upper Peninsula. Her marital partnership with Joe morphed into a formidable, bi-peninsular political force. Supported by tribal resources and a legion of volunteers from Joe's power center in central lower Michigan, the couple forged a campaign that overwhelmed their opponents in the August 2022 Democratic primary.

The political excitement stirred by their energetic base attracted statewide attention and carried Joe to an upset win over the Republican incumbent in the 2022 November general election. Velvet reveled in Joe's victory. When asked by a reporter for her reaction to his win, Velvet replied, "This was a win for those who love our land and our people. This was a win for Gitche Gumee!"

But while Velvet was busy writing thank-you letters to their key supporters, Joe's win stirred speculation among Michigan Democrats that his political journey had only just begun. When asked by reporters if he had higher political ambitions, Joe dodged the question with a standard line: "The voters elected me to represent them in Congress, and that is my sole priority for the next two years."

Baptized into a political world she had once eschewed by a bruising campaign, Velvet looked forward to working with Joe to promote environmental issues in Congress. But she soon learned that the togetherness she had experienced on the campaign trail drifted away now that he had become Congressman-elect Joe Johnson.

Media interviews and party meetings kept Joe away for countless days, further straining their marriage. Velvet might get but a single phone call from Joe during the day, and sometimes she didn't even receive that. She grew accustomed to his coming home late at night, exhausted by the pace of his day. The days of joint travel and exciting conversations became watching newscasts alone and fielding calls from political figures and the press wanting to talk to an absent Joe.

She reluctantly accepted this new relationship, but it was a harsh reality. She hoped their new life in Washington would return them to the campaign togetherness that Joe had promised.

* * *

When they arrived in Washington in January, Joe jumped feet first into the political world, basking in the political spotlight his First American status carried. He eagerly accepted all meetings and interviews and relished the attention thrust upon him. Political events that Joe deemed "necessary" routinely replaced dinner plans or even an evening of watching television together.

"Be patient, Velvet. Things will get easier after I am better known in Congress," he assured her.

But the days turned to weeks, and still there was no letup in his politi-cal pace. His staff was constantly packing his daily schedule, leaving precious little time for her.

"I'll have some personal time scheduled just for us," Joe responded when she asked to be included in his daily schedule.

But all too often, even when they had personal time scheduled, the phone would ring and she soon would find herself alone again, staring out her tiny Alexandria apartment window and dreaming of the U.P.

Velvet phoned Wenonah regularly for support during those lonely early days when Joe was away. "Wenonah, does this get any better—and when?" she asked her sister in desperation.

"Hang in there, sis. Just give Joe a little more time to climb his way up the political ladder. Try to meet the wives and make some friends," Weno-nah counseled.

She tried, but the alien Washington political world was not kind to Velvet. Congressional wives looked at her green headband and wraparound skirts and saw an unsophisticated and undesirable addition to the Wash-ington elite society. Her only personal interaction with them was when she accompanied Joe to political events. Even then, the conversations were only about Joe, despite his attempts to bring her into the conversations.

Inevitably, she slipped into the background of political events as Joe worked the room, eventually drifting into a corner surrounded by insuf-ferable staffers trying to sound important. Worse yet, she couldn't escape those miserable events through drinking, since she had a general distaste for alcohol.

After taking a cab home alone after an uncomfortable social event on St. Patrick's Day, Velvet decided she had had enough.

She waited up for him until the wee hours of the morning.

When he finally came home, a determined Velvet met him with a stern face.

"What's up, Velvet?" Joe asked, sensing something was wrong.

"Where have you been?"

"Just talking with some colleagues about legislation I want to push through committee before the summer break. Got to make the most of this opportunity, as right now people are really listening to me."

Velvet frowned, and then looked him in the eyes.

"Joe, I have tried, but it's not working. I want to go home."

"Now Velvet, I know Washington is not the Upper Peninsula of Michigan but …"

"I am leaving for Christmas tomorrow. I already made a plane reservation, and I'm going home," Velvet declared.

"How will it look if you leave me in D.C. on such short notice? Can you imagine the stories in the local papers?" Joe protested.

"I don't care what the press or anyone in Washington thinks. This is not like it was on the campaign trail. This is not what you promised our life would be. I feel so alone. It's time for me to go back home," she responded.

"What can I do to change your mind, Velvet?"

"I'm sorry, but I've decided. I'm leaving tomorrow," she replied.

"OK, I understand you need to go home for a while, and I know lately I've not been a very attentive partner. As soon as I get some of my legislation passed, things will get better."

"Uh huh," Velvet huffed in disbelief.

"Well, will you at least come back for major events like my first fundraiser?"

"Joe, you know I'll do all I can to help you. It's just that I get so lonely on those long days and nights when you're working, and I have no one to talk to except Wenonah. And even she is sometimes too busy to talk."

"And—" Joe began, but Velvet interrupted him again.

"Joe, I'll see you often in Christmas, since you'll be making trips home to prepare for your re-election. Christmas can be your home base, and we can be together on weekends and stay in touch by phone during the week."

Recognizing there was nothing he could say or do to change her mind, Joe bowed to her wishes. They spent an intimate night together, the first in many weeks. It was as though they were on a second honeymoon, as their night together sparked a physical passion their relationship had lacked since their wedding night.

On her flight to Christmas the next day, she felt her relationship with Joe had been renewed, and a warm feeling came over her. She knew she had made the right move. I'm going back to the home I know, the people I love, and the land that I cherish, she told herself.

But her hope that returning home would improve their marital relationship quickly dissipated. Though Joe made almost weekly trips back to the district, the sheer size of the new district meant that most of his trips were to the more populous counties in the Lower Peninsula and not to Christmas.

And then there was the 2023 Escanaba shooting incident during a campaign rally after Joe had been in office for only five months. Joe had taken the stage and was about to speak when an older, white-haired man in the audience pulled out a pistol and rushed the stage towards Joe. Taylor, who had accompanied Joe, jumped from his chair and dove at the man, taking a bullet in the abdomen as he struggled to restrain him. Taylor crumpled to the ground but refused to release his grip on the gunman's pistol until the assailant was subdued by a security guard.

Taylor was rushed to a nearby hospital, and the doctors said his athletic conditioning had saved him, as a less fit man would not have survived.

However, after a brief pause to address security issues, Joe's trips back to the district resumed, but still with very few to Christmas.

Alone again, Velvet sighed. But at least I am where I want to be.

Meanwhile, Joe set a torrid pace for legislative accomplishments in his first year in Congress. He co-authored a bill awarding a huge environmental grant for Northern Michigan University, an achievement which curried great favor with the science faculty who saw their research funding triple. He also co-authored an educational scholarship program for college students in rural areas of the nation, which reaped significant benefits for many of his younger constituents.

However, his most noteworthy achievement was sponsoring an amendment to a huge Department of Interior authorization bill, which prohibited destructive tribal casino competition on federal lands in rural Michigan. Tribal leaders throughout the district marveled at his legislative adroitness, particularly how it so contrasted with the back-handed treatment they had experienced from the previous incumbent.

In short, he hit a home run for his district in record time and was considered a shoo-in for reelection in 2024. Velvet hoped his success would mean less time needed for campaigning and more time with her. The newspaper headlines and positive press showcasing his legislative success were paying the political dividends he had hoped.

But his success also fueled his higher political ambitions. A headline in a local newspaper two days before Christmas quoted party sources touting Joe for Governor in 2026. The headline shook her, and she called Joe and asked him point-blank if the headline was true.

Joe deflected her question. "There will be plenty of time to talk about all this when I get home tomorrow on Christmas Eve."

* * *

From a weather perspective, it was a strange Christmas holiday in Christmas, Michigan.

Festive spirits in the tiny town, best known for its small casino and a giant cutout Santa Claus mounted outside the local post office, were dampened by a snowless December so rare for Michigan's Upper Peninsula.

High snowbanks and ice-glazed power lines were nowhere to be seen. Instead, there was a lifeless landscape of brown grass and leaf deprived trees.

But Joe was coming home for the Christmas holiday at last, so Velvet ignored the unusual weather and fantasized how she would reunite with him, far from the maddening political crowd.

When Joe arrived at noon on Christmas Eve, he found a warm and inviting holiday home. Velvet had decorated the house with garlands and white twinkling lights. The fireplace was lit, with the logs crackling and a new green comforter on the bed in the freshly painted bedroom.

Velvet rushed to Joe as he opened the front door, and they embraced without talking. She hugged him tightly. It finally was going to be as he had promised, Velvet thought.

While lying together on the couch discussing plans for the night and Christmas Day, the ringing of Joe's cell phone interrupted the couple's conversation.

"Let it ring," Velvet pleaded.

"Let me just check to see if this is urgent," he replied.

Glancing at the number of the caller, Joe took the call and uttered words she did not want to hear.

"Now? Christmas Eve. Can't this wait? It's the first time I have been home with my wife in almost a month," Joe shouted over the phone.

Velvet had heard the story before. There was always someone needing a piece of Joe. And she knew who always won this tug of war.

"All right."

Joe hung up the phone and turned to Velvet with a pained expression.

"No, no, no!" she shouted, recognizing what his next words were likely to be. "This is our time together."

Joe explained there was a last-minute, surprise event to honor a prominent tribal official in Houghton, a small town in the remote western region of his sprawling district.

"I need to go, as my tribal support from the Western Upper Peninsula in the 2022 election was not as solid as it needs to be to discourage serious challengers from that part of the district."

"But you receive so many requests. What's so special about this one? And why now, after you promised to be with me for Christmas?"

Joe started to answer, but Velvet would not let this slide. "Everyone says you are a shoo-in for re-election. You can go there any other time, but not at the last minute and not on Christmas Eve!" she cried.

"Well, Connie, the state Democratic Party Chair, is going to be there as well. She arranged this, so I really can't say no," Joe argued.

Velvet stared at him in silence. How could he do this?

Seeing Joe was standing firm, Velvet shifted tactics.

"Anyway, how in the world are you going to get there on Christmas Eve?"

"The Party chartered a plane for me out of a private airport in Munising. I'll have to leave now to get to the event by dinnertime."

While he marched upstairs to change his clothes, a weather bulletin interrupted the Christmas music playing on the radio. A blizzard watch posted earlier for the Western Upper Peninsula was now upgraded to a warning.

"Joe, you can't go. There's a blizzard warning out west," she shouted up the stairs.

Joe raced downstairs and tuned the radio to the weather station. It confirmed a blizzard warning, but it was not to take effect until after 9 p.m.

"I'll be flying back home before it hits Houghton," Joe assured her.

"I have a bad feeling about this trip," Velvet warned, remembering the storm that took the lives of her parents. "Please don't leave me alone, tonight of all nights. Tribal leaders will understand."

"I've been seriously thinking about a run for Governor in 2026, Velvet, and I won't let a weather prediction endanger it. If I am going to run for governor, and I'm not saying I will, events like this are crucial."

"What?" Velvet exclaimed. "We haven't even talked about you running for governor."

"Velvet, it's only a possibility. I first must win re-election in 2024. After that, we can talk about what lies ahead. And I'll only run with your approval."

Velvet was relieved that his decision was not set in stone. But the sting of another political hurdle did not sit well.

"There will be some very well-connected tribal members there who can help me carry counties in the western U.P. I lost in 2022. And I don't want to disappoint Connie, who arranged the meeting."

Connie's name had come up several times before during their campaign trips, but Velvet didn't consider that to be unusual considering her position in the party. However, Joe seemed particularly concerned about not disappointing Connie today, and Velvet resented that Connie's wishes took priority over his promise to be home with her.

Velvet continued pleading, but her words fell on deaf ears. Joe gave her a hug and assured her he would be home by 10 pm. Since he had no time to enlist the services of his field staff, he left for the airport alone in a rental car to catch a chartered plane at 3:30 pm.

Velvet spent the rest of the day listening to Christmas music on the radio, but frequently switched to the weather station to get updates. She hoped he could beat the storm but remembered being given similar hollow assurances at Whitefish Point years ago.

Eager for his return, she left an hour early that evening to pick him up. Sitting in her car, she stared at the deserted airport runway, dreaming of how the rest of the night would unfold. Just before 10 pm on Christmas Eve, she received a phone call from Joe's western district office manager.

"Mrs. LeBlanc, I am so sorry to report that gale force winds forced your husband's plane off course and into Lake Superior near Marquette around 9:15 pm. The Coast Guard has dispatched a rescue team to find him and the plane."

"What?" Velvet cried. "Haven't they found the plane yet? Is Joe OK?"

"They tracked the plane on radar but lost it after it veered off course. I'm afraid that's all I know," the staffer replied solemnly.

Velvet felt a lump in her throat and a torrent of pent-up emotion paralyzed her voice

Moments passed in silence.

"Mrs. LeBlanc, are you there?" the staffer asked.

Summoning all her strength, she replied, "Yes, call me when you know more," tears rolling down her cheeks.

Though the rescue mission was ongoing, Velvet feared the worst. First her parents and her uncle, and now her husband.

As she sat at the airport parking lot awaiting a plane she knew would not arrive, she felt the same raw emptiness she had experienced at Whitefish Point years ago. A flood of memories raced through her mind like a freight train, but the chilly evening brought her back to reality. She turned on the car ignition for heat.

This is not Whitefish Point and I am not going to just sit here and wait, she resolved. Putting the car in gear, she drove north on a two-track road until she reached the Lake Superior shoreline. Jumping out of her car, she ran to the beach. She stared at the vast expanse of water and cursed the icy arms that sought to claim another loved one.

"Don't forsake me again, Gichi-Gami!" Velvet exclaimed, using the Ojibwe pronunciation of the Big Sea. "Have I not been your servant and protector? Have I not given you my all? Yet still you seek to punish and torment me."

"Why?" she shouted.

"Why?" she repeated softly.

But there was no answer, as Gitche Gumee's waves slapped against the beach.

She sat on the cold beach sand, waiting for the pain to subside, the icy wind stinging her eyes and cheeks.

But the pain continued like a knife twisting in her womb, as she struggled to absorb the likely loss of yet another loved one.

Just then, her phone rang. It was Joe's western district office manager again.

"Mrs. LeBlanc, I am so sorry to report that the search for the Congressman has been suspended because of the high winds and darkness."

She knew the rest of the familiar story and cut him off.

"Call me when you hear anything else, no matter what time it is," she sobbed and ended the call.

She stood up from the beach, brushing the sand off her clothes, and stiffly turned towards her car.

Thoughts of losing Joe grew into her second guessing her entire political journey with him. Was our marriage a mistake and our campaign meaningless, she asked herself? Did we make much of a difference?

She had flashbacks to the events after the November 2022 election. Yes, Joe won the election. And yes, together they lined up First American financial support and built a strong grassroots campaign by organizing students and environment groups, she remembered. But the overall political environment in northern Michigan was still as hostile to their campaign issues as it was before they began their political journey together.

Line 5 still pumped petroleum under the straits, and the policies of many elected Michigan politicians in Lansing remained anti-environment and anti-tribal.

Legislative efforts at the state level to break the monopoly of the 12 tribal casinos operating in her district continued. Will our fragile coalition fall apart if Joe is dead? Will his death signal the end of our environmental journey?

Maybe I never belonged in politics. Maybe I never should have even started.

But she paused before walking back to her car and glanced back at Gitche Gumee, the moonlight reflecting wildly off its choppy surface. For a moment, she felt drawn to its glistening water and a desire to join her husband and her family in its arms.

She kicked off her shoes and slowly walked towards the water's edge, chanting the words of a prayer she had learned as a child:

Oh, Great Spirit, whose voice I hear in the winds

And whose breath gives life to everyone,

Hear me.

I come to you as one of your many children.

But just as her feet touched the icy cold water, she heard a screeching sound and the flapping of wings overhead. Looking up, she saw a large owl circling overhead, which then swooped down and landed on the beach only a few footsteps away.

The owl's eyes glared at her as it unleased a thunderous cry.

Velvet jumped back from the water as the owl began walking towards her. She remembered from Abequa's stories about the owl as a symbol of death and realized she had been sent a message.

Joe was dead.

She need not await a formal announcement.

But she now knew she was not alone. The Great Spirit had not abandoned her and Gitche Gumee was not calling her home.

She scooped up her shoes and headed back to her car.

I must go back to Christmas and await another sign from the Great Spirit for what new journey lies ahead, she thought.

She turned to face down the owl, but it had disappeared.

CHAPTER FIVE

Funeral Pledges

"In politics you must always keep running with the pack. The moment that you falter, and they sense that you are injured, the rest will turn on you like wolves."

—R.A. Butler, British author

SAULT STE. MARIE, MICHIGAN
WINTER, 2024

JOE'S REMAINS WASHED ASHORE ON NEW YEAR'S DAY, A MILE WEST OF Marquette. It had been a long waiting period for Velvet, who feared his body, like the bodies of her parents, would forever rest beneath the waves of Gitche Gumee.

An avalanche of condolence cards and letters overwhelmed the tiny Christmas post office, signaling the need for a funeral venue larger than the local church where they had been married. Frank arranged for Joe's funeral to be held at the newly renovated Kewadin Casino auditorium in the Soo.

But the discovery of his body raised another issue: where to bury him?

Velvet wanted Joe buried at the old Mission Hill Cemetery with her parents.

However, Joe's will directed that he be buried on Mackinac Island, a natural bridge between the two Michigan peninsulas which his district straddled. A political ally had already donated a rare island burial plot to satisfy Joe's wishes.

As a compromise, Joe's body was buried on Mackinac Island, but Velvet had a headstone placed in the old Mission Hill Cemetery to keep him in her spiritual family home.

Sadly, Velvet faced fierce island opposition to Joe's burial on the island and called on Wenonah to overcome resistance by local authorities. It would take a lot of political wrangling to bury a First American from downstate in an exclusive and the highly restricted island cemetery.

Wenonah negotiated a compromise that allowed Joe's burial in the island plot, but only with a simple brass plate resting flat on the ground marking his grave—no visible headstone. The compromise also prevented erecting a spirit house for him.

"Racism continues, even to the grave!" Velvet gasped after learning from her sister about the burial restrictions.

Even after the burial battle was over, the frozen ground prevented the internment of Joe's body. His body would have to rest in a morgue in St Ignace until the spring thaw.

The funeral was held on a cold Wednesday morning in mid-January. Michigan's Republican Governor attended, as did many members of Michigan's Congressional delegation, local officeholders, tribal and environmental leaders, and students. It was a memorial service of sadness despite Velvet's request to celebrate his life rather than mourn his passing.

Velvet overheard politicians at the funeral talking about Joe's death not as losing a colleague but as a new and unexpected political opportunity.

A rare opening for the politically ambitious. She was appalled by their crass comments but determined to get through the service with grace and avoid a confrontation.

After a long procession of well-wishers left the casino, the Governor asked Velvet to meet with him privately in a small room opposite the auditorium. He, along with his chief of staff, offered Velvet their condolences and then delivered a most unexpected proposition.

The chief of staff began by explaining to her that, according to the U.S. Constitution and Michigan law, the Governor would have to call a special election to fill Joe's seat. "I was thinking about scheduling the election to coincide with the Michigan primary in August, but that date is just too long to leave the seat vacant," the Governor explained. "So, I have decided that the election should take place in April—perhaps around Tax Day. The timetable would be very short, with party primaries held in March followed by an April special election to fill the last eight months of Joe's term."

Then the Governor looked directly at Velvet and echoed the sentiments expressed by virtually all in attendance at the funeral: "I think you should run and finish Joe's term."

His proposal startled Velvet, especially since it came from the top Republican in the state.

"I can guarantee no significant Republican opposition to your candidacy if you are the Democratic nominee, and I can steer financial contributions to your campaign. You should win the special election handily."

But then he delivered his quid pro quo. "But I would like Jack to get another crack at winning back his old seat in the Fall; so, I would expect you not to seek your party's nomination in the August 2024 primary. I prefer an open seat if he makes the plunge again."

Velvet just stared at him. What an inappropriate time for such a statement, she thought! The insensitive nature of this proposition stunned her, essentially making her an immediate lame duck with no opportunity to run for Joe's seat in the November election.

Even more infuriating was the idea that she would pave the way for the vanquished Republican incumbent to return to his old seat and resume his assault on the environment and the First American community.

Her first instinct was to lash out. But again, the somber occasion dictated otherwise. Instead, she demurred and said she would get back to him after her pain subsided.

"I understand, Evangeline," the Governor nodded in agreement.

But he pressed on.

"Let me know by the end of next week, as I have a couple of hungry young wolves eager to jump in to fill this vacancy, and I need to give them a heads up before they publicly declare their candidacies and complicate the April special election."

Wolves, she thought. The Governor is worried about his party's wolves while she is mourning the loss of her husband. Her sadness morphed into anger, as she once again experienced the heartlessness of the political world and the craven politicians who populated it.

This was not the time to worry about his political wolves, she thought.

She had a major decision to make in her very young political life. She could either emerge from Joe's shadow and seize the political mantle of leadership in the district, or quietly fill out the rest of his term and return to life in Christmas.

There must be strong public support for me for the Republican Governor to make this offer, she thought. But can I win with my limited political experience and few resources?

Is this the journey the Great Spirit wants me to take?

There was one person she trusted to give her the political counsel she needed. So, after the Governor left, she texted Wenonah, who could guide her through the politics of the situation as well as understand her personal misgivings.

Wenonah was being interviewed by a local reporter in the casino lobby after the funeral service when she received Velvet's text.

"Please meet me at the auditorium?"

Wenonah broke off the interview and rushed to her sister.

"I'm on my way," she texted.

When Wenonah arrived at the auditorium entrance, the pair walked across to the small room where Velvet had held her previous conversation with the Governor.

Velvet described her frustration with the Governor's conversation.

"I don't know if I even want to run for Joe's seat. I haven't yet come to grips with losing him, much less replacing him. But I resent the Governor pressing me to decide this very day."

Wenonah nodded. It was an unfair and unfeeling move by the Governor. But fair or not, there was not a lot of time for Velvet to ponder her political future before this window of opportunity closed.

"My Michigan political friends tell me you have a very good chance to win the special election, with or without the Governor's support," Wenonah asserted. "But whether you are willing to take on the personal challenges ahead is something only you can decide."

Seeing Velvet still troubled, she continued. "Call some of Joe's key supporters? You know, the ones you have known even before the campaign. Ask them whether they would support you. If they equivocate or advise against a run for the seat, you have your answer, as you will need their support for such a campaign," Wenonah counseled.

"What would you do if you were in my place, Wenonah?" Velvet pressed.

"Look, I know from my experience in the political world that opportunities like this are rare. Unlike you, Velvet, I always dreamed of running for political office, but the Great Spirit sent me down a different path. I really can't complain though, as my K Street lobbying has been politically and financially rewarding."

Wenonah paused, and Velvet saw in Wenonah's face that her deeper emotions were now coming out.

"Velvet, I know this is not the journey you sought when you married Joe. But you have come so far from my little sister from Christmas, Michigan, to the threshold of becoming the first, First American Congresswoman from Michigan."

Velvet gazed at Wenonah and saw the sincerity in her eyes as Wenonah continued.

"Velvet, if you run, do it because you want to. Don't run for Joe's sake. You can do this! I know you can, and I will be with you all the way. You are my strong little sister, and this is your moment if you choose to seize it!"

Wenonah paused.

"I see the hand of the Great Spirit leading you down this new path."

The two sisters embraced, with both in tears recognizing this consequential moment in both of their lives.

"What should I tell the Governor?" Velvet asked.

"Screw him," Wenonah snorted.

Velvet smiled.

"There's no guarantee the Governor will deliver on his promises anyway," she continued.

"Just have a private telephone conversation with him and tell him you are considering running in the special election, but it is not your intention AT THIS TIME to run for Joe's seat in the August primary," Wenonah advised.

Use that exact language, Wenonah argued, and you can forestall any early Republican challengers and buy time to decide whether to seek a full two-year term.

With Wenonah at her side, she called the Governor, telling him she may well run in the special election and that she would make an announcement soon. She accepted his proposal of support for her candidacy in the words composed by Wenonah.

The Governor thanked her for the call and promised he would go to work right away to discourage major Republican opposition in the special election.

After hanging up, Velvet called Amy, Joe's trusted press secretary, and described her conversation with the Governor. Would Amy stick with her if she ran for Joe's seat?

Amy assured Velvet she was all in.

With that assurance, she asked Amy to schedule a meeting with Joe's staff on Monday morning, when she would announce her plans for Joe's seat in the April special election.

She also asked Amy to text her the phone numbers of key tribal and student environmental leaders in the district. She planned to contact as many of them as possible as soon as possible.

Taylor had offered to drive her home to Christmas after the funeral. So, after giving Wenonah a hug, she texted him to pick her up at the Soo casino entrance. It would be a long ride from the Soo, so she took Wenonah's advice and used the time to call those she most trusted. Knowing Taylor's close connection with many of these same people, she put her calls on speaker phone.

"Taylor, would you listen to their responses and tell me whether they sound sincere?" Velvet asked.

"Sure!" Taylor replied.

The overwhelmingly positive responses she received from Joe's former supporters truly heartened Velvet. She saw through the rearview mirror Taylor's smiling and wide-eyed response to each supporter's unequivocal endorsement. It gave her the reassurance she needed.

When they pulled up to her driveway, she paused before getting out of the car and asked Taylor a pointblank question. "Taylor, will you help me in a special election congressional campaign if I decide to run?"

"I will do whatever is best for you," was his response.

His statement seemed unnecessarily nuanced, but maybe she was being too analytical, she thought.

Upon walking into her house, a familiar warmth enveloped her. It was as though her parents had met her at the door and hugged her. This is the right thing to do, she said to herself. This is my new journey forward.

She grabbed her phone and called Amy. "No need to wait until the Monday staff meeting to announce my intentions," she said. "I'm all in for the April special election."

"It will be a sprint and not a cakewalk campaign," Amy warned, as it was less than two months until the Democratic primary in March and only one more month until the special election in April.

But Velvet felt an adrenalin rush akin to the feelings she had during her first campaign with Joe: focused and excited. She asked Amy to arrange a meeting with several key Sault tribal council members for the next morning in the Soo. The first campaign conversation of her campaign was going to be with her most trusted friends and allies.

She spent the rest of the daydreaming about how things would be if she were in charge, and then endured a night filled with ghostly visions of her parents and Joe.

Taylor arrived at her home early the next morning, ready to drive her to the tribal meeting in the Soo.

"How do you think they will receive me, Taylor?" Velvet asked.

"Frank will be there to greet you, so how could it be anything other than a warm welcome?" Taylor responded.

Knowing that she would not be alone eased Velvet's anxiety. Upon their arrival at the casino hotel, a small delegation of tribal members headed by Frank met her and applauded as she stepped out of the car. It was an upbeat start for an important day, and her excitement grew.

The welcoming party ushered her into the board of directors' chamber, where she received a standing ovation. She gushed at the attention.

So, this is what politicians thrive upon. I get it now, she thought.

She paused before stepping up to the podium, modestly but happily absorbing the attention thrust upon her. After the applause ended and all were seated, Velvet thanked them all for their past support of Joe. Then her words became more solemn. She began by reading from a script she had written on her morning ride to the meeting.

"You know what an uphill battle a First American faces in this district, much less a First American woman. I need your support even more than Joe did. We can't let the pawn of the mining interests that Joe defeated in 2022 get back into office and threaten our casinos—our new buffaloes, so to speak."

She paused, looking at all the directors. "Can we?"

"No!" the council members shouted spontaneously.

Velvet set aside her script and seized the emotional moment. "Are you with me? Are you ready to stand with me as you did with Joe?" she asked rhetorically, raising her voice.

The tribal board of directors' responses were swift and unequivocal. One by one, each of the directors signaled their full support with shouts and pumped fists.

Taylor was sitting outside the chamber and heard the roar from the directors.

When Velvet emerged from the chamber a few minutes later, Taylor rushed to her side.

"Well?"

Velvet just smiled and signaled for him to lead the way to the car. Frank had an animated conversation with Velvet as they walked behind him, but Taylor couldn't make out their words.

Then Frank gave Velvet a big hug and offered some additional words of encouragement.

When Velvet got in the car and the door slammed, Taylor, who was now sitting in the driver's seat, repeated his question.

"Well?"

"I can't believe how easy my first campaign pitch was," she gushed.

"It's not always going to be this easy, you know. This group supported you already," Taylor cautioned. "But," he added, "I never heard Joe get such a rousing ovation!"

Velvet beamed with pride.

Word of her solid support from the powerful Sault tribe won over all but the most skeptical local Democratic leaders who were still smarting from the failed 2020 campaign of their anointed candidate. The emotional edge of her campaign just might make Velvet the right candidate to keep the seat blue, at least until November. So, word went out to all potential Democratic contenders in the March primary that the fix was in for Velvet.

Now, Velvet thought, if the Governor would just deliver on his promise of money and no serious competition from his party, my pathway to victory in the special election is assured.

So that evening she called the Governor from her casino hotel room to confirm that she would run for Joe's seat and ask that he confirm his offer of support.

The Governor's reply unnerved her.

"Evangeline, you know I can't publicly endorse you; but I will privately try to discourage other challengers. I will tell the party regulars I will not campaign in the special election. And I'll contact some of my private donors and tell them I will turn a blind eye to any contributions they may wish to make to your campaign."

The Governor paused, waiting for her to respond.

But Velvet did not respond, leaving a long and uncomfortable silence.

Then he finally interjected the word, "OK?"

"Not OK," Velvet responded. "I need your public support to stave off your party regulars."

"Evangeline, it is clear you don't understand party politics, or you wouldn't be asking me to commit political suicide. Now just be happy with my help behind the scenes and get ready to go back to D.C."

Velvet did not respond.

"Now I have other calls I have to make, so good luck Congresswoman LeBlanc," he responded, and hung up the phone.

His meager offer of conditional, behind-the-scenes support was not what she expected.

After taking a deep breath, she checked her phone to see if any new messages had come in during their conversation. She had received several more voice mail messages of support from Joe's allies, but she was still worried about the Governor.

She called Wenonah.

"Wenonah, I just got off the phone with the Governor who is backpedaling on his promises. Do I really need him?"

Wenonah, who had been skeptical all along that party leaders—especially Republican ones—would back her sister, replied with a single word response: "Nope!"

She then outlined a plan to use the skills of Velvet's young supporters on social media rather than more traditional and expensive television and radio buys to get her message across and reduce reliance on campaign contributions from the Governor's donors.

"And what about my running for re-election in November?" Velvet continued. "If I don't need him, should I tell him now that I will not be a short termer?"

"No need to show your hand now," Wenonah counseled. "One step at a time."

"But I want the satisfaction of telling him the deal is off," Velvet protested.

"Look, Velvet, if he can play word games, so can you. Let him think he's won this round for his pal Jack and take his meager offer of help while we develop our campaign strategy."

Velvet nodded, agreeing Wenonah's advice was politically wiser, but she would have preferred her own approach.

Wenonah paused and smiled. "Now let's get you elected."

CHAPTER SIX

Hail, Hail The Gang's All Here

"The U.S. Congress is now run by paid staffers,
not by people elected to do the job."

—Barry Goldwater

SAULT STE. MARIE, MICHIGAN
SPRING, 2024

"WILL JOE'S STAFF STICK WITH YOU?" WENONAH ASKED

Velvet had not considered that possibility. Joe's experienced campaign staff was an invaluable resource, but was their loyalty only to Joe?

"I'll ask Taylor," Velvet replied. "He would know who might leave."

"Be discreet and talk with him alone and in person. You're an excellent reader of people's faces, so look him directly in the eye when you ask him."

"I think Taylor would be honest, but I agree that a one-on-one conversation would be best," Velvet responded. "I'll talk with him first thing in the morning," she replied, ending the call and flopping on a bed that had become a second home for her at the Soo casino.

Overnight she devised a plan for meeting with Taylor alone, texting him and copying Joe's press secretary Amy with the following message: "Taylor, can you drive me to St. Ignace? Joe's body will stay in the morgue until spring. I want to say goodbye before I leave for D.C. to meet Joe's staff."

She then sat down and compiled a list of staff members whom she felt she had to keep, including Amy, Angela, the assistant press secretary, and Jim Zenger, Joe's field staff director. Velvet hoped she could keep all of Joe's staff.

About an hour after her text, a soft knock on her hotel room door awakened her.

When she opened the door, she was surprised to see both Amy and Taylor. Velvet wanted Taylor's frank assessment, suspecting there was some tension between Taylor and Amy, which made Amy's presence problematic.

"Amy, I need you to call some key state Democratic party leaders and create a list of who my likely opponents might be in the special election." It was a spur-of-the-moment request that she hoped would give her some time alone with Taylor. "Taylor can drive me to St. Ignace while you make the calls; and when I return, we'll go over your list."

"I can make those calls in the car on our way to St. Ignace," Amy protested.

"No, I prefer you make the calls with no distractions. I will explain later. Just trust me."

Velvet could tell Amy was unhappy, but she didn't want to mislead Amy by further spinning her carefully worded request. Smiling, she handed Amy her hotel room card and beckoned Taylor to accompany her down the hall to the elevator.

After the elevator doors closed, Velvet pulled out a list of Joe's campaign staff she had compiled. "Taylor, would you look over this list and cross off anyone you think shouldn't be part of my campaign?"

She watched Taylor's face as he glanced at the list. He looked troubled. Rather than stare at him while he read the list, Velvet turned away and phoned a key, friendly state legislator to advise him of her decision to run. Getting a voice mail message and with the elevator door opening to the lobby, she ended the call, and they exited the elevator.

Taylor handed back her list with only three names stricken from her list—Joe's administrative assistant, Amy, and Jim Zenger—the latter two being staff members that Velvet had most wanted to keep.

"Trust me, it will better serve you if these three are not on your staff," Taylor warned.

Velvet understood why he had struck the name of Joe's administrative assistant, as he had been applying for jobs elsewhere after he and Joe had strongly disagreed over office spending priorities.

It also did not surprise her he struck Amy's name, as it seemed to confirm rumors that there was or had been something going on between Taylor and Amy. But she did not press the issue.

But his opposition to Jim Zenger was unexpected. What could possibly be Taylor's concern? Jim had been a regular companion with Joe throughout the latter part of his first campaign and had accompanied Joe on his district trips when Velvet could not attend.

Jim, a tall Polish American from the Detroit area, was well-connected with state party officials, including Connie, the state Democratic party chair. He was a talented political strategist with an aggressive personality. At the young age of thirty-one, he had already run two successful state legislative campaigns, and his energy was contagious. Impeccably dressed and an exercise fanatic, Jim was the perfect image for her youthful supporters and an important political link to the state party for her fledgling campaign.

"Taylor, Amy has been with us since Joe and I began our campaign. We'll have to talk about her some more, but why Jim?"

Taylor paused and then gave what she felt was an evasive response.

"Let's just say that Jim and I do not see eye to eye on campaign management, and I think someone new would better serve you to run your field operations," Taylor responded, avoiding direct eye contact with Velvet.

"Oh?" she responded.

She recognized the tension in his face. Was he holding back something important? They proceeded in silence to St. Ignace, but she had a gnawing feeling in her gut. Was Taylor hiding a damning secret, or was he signaling his lack of confidence in her campaign?

She knew she could not dismiss Amy. She had known Amy first as a reporter for the *Sault Evening News*. Her stories about environmental issues and the favorable coverage she gave to her protest rallies forever endeared her to Velvet.

At 36 and single, Amy was a heavy-set woman who carried her weight well through a combination of smart dressing and careful grooming. At five feet two inches tall, the press might overlook her in a crowd but for her aggressive personality and booming voice. She was the assertive spokesperson needed for the campaign and not shy about sharing her opinions. She was also politically astute despite her limited geographical upbringing, having moved at age ten from Green Bay, Wisconsin, to the Soo, where she had lived the rest of her young adult life. She caught Joe's eye when she interviewed him and posed some tough, thought-provoking questions.

Most importantly, Amy was well-respected by the First American community, known for her fair and in-depth coverage of tribal casino issues. And her parents were major contributors to the Michigan Democratic party. Those factors led Joe to ask Amy to join his campaign for Congress even before he officially announced his candidacy.

Amy was staying, period. But Jim Zenger was a different issue. Velvet never had a strong personal tie with him like she had with Amy. While he had been a regular companion to Joe on his district trips, Joe treated him more like a political ally than a close friend. And unlike Taylor, Jim never attempted to befriend Velvet nor make any effort to attend the few social events she hosted at her home in Christmas.

But Joe swore Jim was an organizational genius. Party officials believed Jim was the political glue that had held Joe's fragile campaign coalition together.

Why dump Jim Zenger, she kept asking herself?

When they arrived in St. Ignace and pulled up to the morgue, Velvet could no longer hold her thoughts in check. "Taylor, shut off the engine. We have to deal with this staffing issue right now."

He did as she asked, and then stared out the window, struggling to escape her gaze.

"I can't drop Amy and Jim from the campaign unless you give me a more compelling reason to do so. They are simply too important to be left out."

She watched as Taylor's face fell from surprise to sadness as her words sank in.

He turned and looked directly at Velvet.

"Here's my problem with Amy. I hooked up with her once, which I feel has complicated our working relationship. I know you need a campaign with no distractions, and I worry our past might be a problem."

Velvet shook her head in disagreement.

Pausing, Taylor then continued. "But now that you know this, I will try my best to work with her through December, if you need us both," Taylor offered.

"I do need both of you. Please do this for me."

Taylor nodded in agreement.

"All right. So, what's the problem with Jim?"

"Jim represents the dark side of Joe's campaign. He carries a lot of political baggage that could cripple you," Taylor replied.

"Like what? Be specific!" Velvet pressed in frustration.

"That's all I am comfortable saying," Taylor responded. "You'll just have to trust me. He's not right for your campaign."

"Not good enough, Taylor."

"I cannot work with that guy."

"We'll have to take this up again soon," Velvet replied, ignoring Taylor's warning. She then stepped out of the car and entered the front entrance of the morgue.

She hoped Taylor would change his mind after some reflection, though she still didn't know the root of Taylor's issue with Jim.

Softly whispering a brief prayer to the Great Spirit as she knelt near where Joe's body rested, she bowed her head and prayed for his soul. Then, composing herself after a few moments of reflection, she rose and returned to the car.

The trip back to the Soo was an usually quiet one, as both Velvet and Taylor weighed their options for resolving their staff disagreements.

＊ ＊ ＊

After dropping Velvet off at the Soo casino hotel, Taylor was troubled for being so evasive with Velvet about Jim Zenger, so he took matters into his own hands.

Since Jim already was in the Soo, Taylor texted him a dinner invitation at a restaurant on Portage Street that evening, hoping to convince Jim to leave Velvet's campaign voluntarily.

Jim agreed to dinner and was already at a table when Taylor arrived early that evening.

Good, Taylor thought. Jim seems relaxed. Maybe my pitch will be a little easier. After taking a seat, Taylor got right to the point.

"Jim, I think it's best you don't leave tomorrow with Velvet to line up her campaign staff."

Taylor saw Jim's eyes widen, but before Jim could reply, Taylor delivered another body blow.

"And I think you should call her tonight, wish her well, and tell her you will not be joining her campaign."

Jim's facial expression then changed from surprise to a sly smile.

"Well, thank you, Taylor, for your sage political advice, but I think I'm the best judge of what my plans will be. Did Velvet send you or is this your idea?"

Taylor ignored the last question and continued.

"I know what you and Joe have been doing on your district trips, and I don't want those things to become public and hurt Velvet. If you stay with the campaign and the press finds out about you and Joe, it will destroy Velvet."

"Do you think I'm a fool?" Jim shot back. "Who's going to leak this story? Not me. If that story got out, it would not be because I stayed on her campaign."

Taylor paused and then leaned forward towards Jim.

"Every day I see your face, I am reminded of what you have done. I want all this to go away so Velvet can build her political career without a potential scandal hanging over her head."

"Political career?" Jim sneered. "You're the fool!"

Jim leaned forward and glared at Taylor, dropping his own bombshell.

"Don't you know the party has no plans to support Velvet after the April special election? She's just a placeholder riding an emotional wave of sympathy. Party officials want a better candidate to represent the party in the August primary, even if Velvet runs for re-election."

Now it was Taylor's turn to be stunned. What the hell! Could this be true?

"Connie asked me to keep a close eye on Velvet while they search for a suitable candidate to run in the Democratic primary in August. No one in the party has any confidence in Velvet's ability to win the seat outright in the November election," Jim scoffed.

"So," Jim continued," I am going to join her special election campaign, which she will win. The fix is on for her nomination. In the meantime, we'll be looking for a different Democratic candidate for the general election. So why don't you crawl back to Velvet like a good boy, shut your mouth about all this, and leave it to us political pros to keep this seat Democratic?"

Taylor stood up, shocked by Jim's callousness, and stormed out of the restaurant, hearing Jim's mocking laughter and welling up with rage.

As he sat in his car parked outside the front door of the restaurant pondering his next steps, rain speckled his windshield. He was not sure whether it was the rain or his emotions that blurred his vision as he stared out his car window. But after a few minutes, he saw Jim emerge from the restaurant, cell phone in hand, engaging it in what looked like a very animated conversation.

If what Jim said was true, he was probably calling Connie, Taylor thought.

Was Jim truthful about plans by the party to dump Velvet after the special election, or was this just a clever mind game he was playing? Taylor sensed Jim was jealous of his close relationship with Velvet.

Maybe Jim contrived the story, hoping I would tell Velvet. Party officials would then deny the story, undermining my relationship with both Velvet and the party. And if I leak it to the press, it could sink her campaign regardless of its truthfulness.

He prayed Jim was lying, but his conversation seemed devilishly genuine.

Now Taylor knew Jim had to go. This malignancy within her campaign had to be excised, as Jim could not be trusted, whether or not his story was true.

Taylor knew Velvet deserved a good reason to dump Jim. Telling her of the alleged party treachery or, worse yet, revealing the dark secret about Joe's district trips with Jim were options too painful to disclose just before the primary.

So he called Velvet that night in one last attempt to change her mind. His personal pleas were unpersuasive, and Velvet seemed firm that Jim's organizational skills were vital to her campaign.

"I can do Jim's job," Taylor finally exclaimed.

"Taylor, I know you mean well, but Joe told me Jim was indispensable during his winning campaign. We have only a couple of months for this campaign, and this is no time for on-the-job training."

Taylor saw he was making no headway using personal appeals to remove Jim. So, he dropped the subject, wished her well on her trip to Washington the next day, and ended their conversation with a few words of encouragement. But he could not sleep thinking about his conversation with Jim.

So, he sat down early the next morning and composed a text to Velvet:

Dear Velvet:

I have been thinking about our campaign staffing conversation, and I think I could better serve you by focusing all my energy on registering and organizing students throughout the district to prepare for the special election.

So, I believe it would be best that I not join your campaign in an official capacity.

I hope my organizational efforts will be helpful to you and other Democrats running for office this year.

Best wishes,

Taylor

I hope she understands that I'm doing this because I care for her and not think I am abandoning her, Taylor thought as he hit the send key. He then left a voice message with her Soo district office, asking them to pick up Velvet that morning.

With that done, he left for Mount Pleasant.

Velvet did not read his message until the next morning, when a new driver arrived at the casino to take her to the airport.

"Where's Taylor?" she asked the driver.

"I don't know, Mrs. LeBlanc," he responded. "I just got a message from the district office that I was to give you a ride to the airport."

Velvet reached for her phone and saw there was a message from Taylor.

Her hands trembled as she read his text.

"No. no, no!" she broke down as she dropped her phone on the car floor.

CHAPTER SEVEN

Tax Day Cometh

There are things of which I may not speak
There are dreams that cannot die;
There are thoughts that make the strong heart weak,
And bring a pallor into the cheek
And a mist before the eye.

—Henry Wadsworth Longfellow

MOUNT PLEASANT, MICHIGAN
APRIL 2024

TAYLOR DROVE BACK TO MOUNT PLEASANT, FEELING HELPLESS TO protect Velvet from the political peril ahead.

It was a four-hour drive from the Soo on a good day, but this was not a good day.

Snow and ice in Gaylord added nearly an hour to the driving time, and Taylor's thoughts of leaving Velvet to the mercy of Jim and Connie or to the press weighed heavily on his mind.

But this is the political world she has chosen, he reminded himself.

I did all I could, he rationalized. To leave the campaign was better for Velvet than disclosing the alleged plot by the party, complicating her chances of winning the special election.

And if Jim's story were true, then staying on the campaign without telling Velvet would make him complicit in the plot.

Besides, she might not want to run for re-election, or she might lose the special election. Then, even if all this scheming by Jim and the party were true, there would be no reason for this betrayal to be disclosed.

Though his anger grew, his withdrawal from the campaign allowed him to focus on keeping his students and their environmental message front and center for the 2024 campaign. He worked with top student activists developing an environmental policy agenda that he hoped Velvet would adopt as part of her campaign message.

Satisfying himself that withdrawal was the only reasonable path to take, Taylor settled back in Mount Pleasant and hoped Velvet, in time, would understand.

But Velvet was not the only one shaken by his departure.

Taylor's departure from her campaign shocked many of Velvet's staff. He was the most popular member of Joe's staff and had been one of Joe's closest aides. As a former student government president and outstanding athlete at Central Michigan University, he had been instrumental in the student voter registration drive in mid-Michigan that was key to Joe's congressional victory in 2022.

Some staffers speculated that Jim Zenger was the reason for Taylor's absence, as many felt he was jealous of Taylor and pushed him out. Others believed it was the guilt Taylor felt because he did not accompany Joe on his fatal flight from Houghton in December.

And then there was always the whispered rumor that Taylor had a secret romantic relationship with a key member of her staff that had soured.

Taylor was aware of all this speculation, but refused to address it, arguing he was supporting Velvet in the best way possible by working the campus circuit.

After finishing the environmental research project, Taylor emailed a summary to Velvet and asked for a meeting to unveil the details of the proposal.

However, Jim was determined to isolate Taylor from the campaign. He established himself as the filter for all external communications to and from Velvet and told her instead that Taylor had been unresponsive to his calls for help or guidance.

He made sure Taylor's email never reached her desk.

Not getting a response after three days, Taylor tried calling Velvet, but Jim changed her cell phone number to further consolidate his access to Velvet. Taylor was forced to place his calls to her through the campaign office, and Jim directed the staff to forward all calls from Taylor to him, which went unanswered.

Finally, in frustration, Taylor called Jim directly.

"Jim, why is no one returning my calls? I want to talk about the environmental policy proposal I emailed her as I think—"

But Jim cut him off.

"Look, Taylor, Velvet is angry that you refused to help her and told me to handle your calls. We already have our campaign messaging in place."

"But," Taylor interjected.

"Sorry, Taylor, but I have my orders, and your proposal is not part of our campaign. No need to call again, pal," Jim responded sarcastically and hung up.

Taylor was shocked. How could Velvet shut him out like that?

He drove from Mount Pleasant throughout the night to get to Christmas and talk with her face to face. But upon arrival in the early morning hours, he discovered her home was now a temporary campaign office, and Velvet was staying in the Soo casino hotel.

Undeterred, he proceeded to the Soo casino but was blocked by hotel security from reaching Velvet on Jim's orders.

Convinced further efforts to contact Velvet would be futile, he returned to Mount Pleasant and began looking for another outlet for his research.

Taylor's environmental policy received a shot in the arm a few days later, when the *Detroit Free Press* published his letter to the editor outlining a new environmental policy for Michigan. The letter generated a flurry of positive online responses and triggered an unusual amount of discussion at the state capitol as well.

More importantly, his research received rave reviews from the state environmental community and was adopted by the Green Party, which was running a long shot, third-party campaign in the April special election. Its congressional nominee was a young woman by the name of Lorraine Sampson, whose efforts to help the city of Flint overcome a lead pipe water crisis years ago made her a heroine in the mid-Michigan area.

Taylor knew Lorraine well, as she had come to the CMU campus several times and spoken at his student environmental forums. Indeed, there were rumors that Taylor had more than a professional relationship with her, though his close friends denied any such relationship.

It pleased him when Lorraine asked to be briefed on his proposal. His research would become part of a congressional campaign, even if Velvet didn't adopt it.

But before going to meet Lorraine, he called a friend in the polling business. "Do you think the Green Party will play a spoiler role in the special election and take enough votes away from Velvet to flip the race to the Republicans?" he asked.

"Not a chance," his friend replied, citing polling data that showed Velvet had a wave of sympathy and united party support that should lead to an easy win in the special election.

Relieved, Taylor traveled to Lorraine's campaign headquarters and had a long and friendly conversation with her. However, when Lorraine asked him to join her campaign, he declined.

"Lorraine, I'm grateful that you will adopt our policy research for your campaign, but I'm still supporting Velvet."

"Why do you stick with her? She obviously rejected your proposal, or you wouldn't be here," Lorraine snapped.

"You and Velvet are both strong environmental advocates, but my heart is still with Velvet. She's very special to me," Taylor responded.

"I think you are hitching your wagon to the wrong horse, Taylor, but I respect your loyalty. Remember, politics is a journey, not a sprint. You need to take the long view, and Velvet is only a flash in the pan."

Lorraine's warning rattled around in Taylor's mind, but his loyalty to Velvet was enough to convince him that refusing to join Lorraine's campaign was the right decision.

Meanwhile, Velvet's campaign was riding a wave of optimism. With tribal financial support, most of Joe's old staff, and a wave of public sympathy, the political consensus was that Velvet was in the driver's seat for the special election.

Velvet's high profile in fighting the Line 5 pipeline gave her a highly charged issue that helped define her campaign. The impact of the 2020 straits oil slick was still lingering in the minds of many voters, as it had adversely affected business and recreation interests along the shoreline communities of her sprawling district. The novelty of being a First American woman and the widow of the late Congressman also gave her valuable free publicity.

And Velvet was fortunate to avoid a costly contested party primary.

Michigan Democratic Party leaders made it clear to potential challengers that Velvet was the anointed one. She could save her precious campaign resources for the general election campaign.

With only a month between the March primary and the April special election, there was not a lot of time for fundraising, anyway. The key, she was told, was to get her supporters out to vote through a social media blitz and a labor-intensive grassroots effort.

Her strongest Republican challenger was not so lucky. The relatively unknown, wealthy business executive from Traverse City had to dig deep into his personal fortune to defeat two local government officials and win his party's nomination.

The March Republican primary gave the Traverse City challenger a strong win, as he garnered nearly 45 percent of the Republican votes, with his two main challengers earning 30 percent and 22 percent, respectively. But now, with a primary win under his belt, he had only one month to unify his Republican support and take on Velvet. He loaned his campaign nearly two million dollars for his primary campaign and pledged to match that amount in the next month, primarily with an expensive media buy district wide.

Although Velvet tallied a respectable number of votes for her virtually uncontested primary, there were new warning signs that the general election would not be the cakewalk experts earlier had predicted.

First, there was concern about the primary vote totals. Because of the low voter turnout in the Democratic primary, the Republican primary had drawn more combined votes than Velvet's primary totals.

Then there was concern about the Governor's support. Velvet received no direct help from the Republican Governor, though she did not face high profile challengers. Would the Governor renege on his promise after seeing the strong Republican vote totals, Velvet worried?

Most worrisome was the popularity of the Green Party in the April special election. Lorraine's adoption of Taylor's environmental agenda had lured several college student leaders to her campaign. While Taylor's effectiveness in organizing a strong student turnout was an advantage for Velvet, erosion of student support in favor of Lorraine's campaign was an unintended negative consequence.

Reports that Velvet was losing student support led pollsters to change their prediction of a Velvet victory from "Solid Democratic" to "Likely Democratic". Since there were no reliable polls from which to judge either the turnout or the ideological bent of likely voters in April, there were still a lot of unknowns.

* * *

Only three days before the April election, a troublesome local newspaper poll of mid-Michigan voters showed a sudden upsurge in student support for Lorraine. Growing support for the Green Party on the CMU campus was a flashing red light for Velvet's campaign.

The poll rattled Velvet and her staff, forcing her to change her campaign schedule so she could spend the last day before the special election in downstate Mount Pleasant instead of in the Soo to shore up her student support.

She held a morning student rally on the CMU campus and was interviewed on CMU Public Television in the afternoon. The campaign capped off her visit by renting a convention room at the Soaring Eagle Casino and Resort to rally Joe's closest supporters and friends.

Her singing highlighted the evening casino rally as she rolled out a vibrant protest song she re-wrote the night before, dedicated to her parents and to her husband, Joe. She entitled the revised song "In the Arms of Gitche Gumee," a song laced with personal stories about how the waves of Lake Superior had shaped her political journey.

It was a good last day for the campaign, and she felt they had turned the tide in her favor. Victory seemed assured.

Later that evening, she slipped down to the casino pool alone and dove in for a brief swim before retiring for the night. There was only a young couple hugging each other at the far end of the large pool, but the man looked strangely familiar. She watched as he pulled himself out of the pool and stared at her.

She gasped. It was Taylor!

She turned and began swimming towards the nearest ladder farthest from Taylor.

But it was too late.

"Velvet!" Taylor shouted as he trotted towards her.

There was no avoiding this meeting now, as she pulled herself out of the pool and forced a smile as he met her at the top of the pool ladder.

There was an awkward silence as they stood face to face for the first time since his departure from her campaign.

Velvet crossed her arms to cover her breasts, as it was uncomfortable to be in this state of undress and so close to Taylor.

As her eyes dropped to avoid his gaze, she noticed for the first time the poorly tattooed "C" on the right side of his chest.

He saw her puzzled look.

"You are wondering about the 'C,' aren't you?"

She nodded.

He explained that on the night CMU won the Mid-American Conference football championship for the first time in many years, the players agreed to be tattooed with the word "CHIPS", the nickname of their team, on a body part of their choosing.

Velvet tried to hide her amusement at the thought of branding a line of half-naked young men.

He explained that several of the players put the word on parts of their body that were well hidden from the naked eye but more painful to endure. Taylor initially thought he would have "Chips" tattooed across his chest. However, while waiting for his turn in line, he saw the pain that his teammates endured and decided not to take part.

He stepped out of the line and reached down to pick up his shirt, but his teammates did not let him out of his pledge. They pinned him to the tattoo table while the tattoo artist struggled to tattoo his chest.

Taylor then raised his right arm over his head and showed Velvet the word "CHIPS" on the underside of his forearm. He explained that the tattoo artist gave up on the chest tattoo after he struggled so energetically against it, despite four teammates holding him down. So, after the tattoo artist finished only the fuzzy letter 'C' on his chest, Taylor agreed not to struggle anymore, provided the word CHIPS was tattooed on his forearm instead.

"That's a good story, Taylor," she smiled

"Not one I am proud of, but it is a great icebreaker at a swim party," he chuckled.

Velvet grinned, but abruptly changed the subject.

"I was so hurt when you chose not to work on my campaign after all we had been through together."

"And it hurt that you blocked me from contacting you afterwards," Taylor countered.

"I did no such thing!" Velvet responded indignantly.

"I should have known he was lying," Taylor mumbled under his breath.

Then he continued, "I tried to get my environmental policy to you, but your staff blocked me at every level."

Velvet frowned. "I don't know what you are talking about."

Realizing Jim had misled him, Taylor asked hopefully, "So you are not angry with me?"

"Never," she replied. "I don't know what happened over the last two months, and I intend to find out after the special election. But I need you back with me. I know we'll win tomorrow."

Then she looked at him face to face and asked, "Will you join me in Washington after this election? I so need someone I can trust."

Taylor stood silently, weighing what his next words should be. If the experts were right that Velvet would win and if Jim were telling the truth, the party's betrayal plan would soon kick in, Taylor feared.

But Velvet continued to press: "Why won't you rejoin me? Is it a romance with a member of the campaign, a feud with Jim, sadness about Joe's death, or … me?"

Taylor could not respond. He turned to walk away, but she grabbed his arm and turned him towards her again. "Is it me?"

Tears ran down his face as he tried to compose an evasive response.

It was an emotional scene for the otherwise composed young man to break down in front of her. She embraced him and he hugged her tightly.

"Please forgive me, Velvet," he cried.

She looked up at him, puzzled by his request for forgiveness.

There was no turning back now. He realized that his ability to protect her would be futile if he failed to be forthright at this tender moment. It was time to reveal the secret he had kept from Velvet and the real reason he wanted Jim Zenger gone.

"Velvet, this is the most difficult thing I've ever had to tell someone I so care for," Taylor began.

She held her breath, fearing his next words.

"Do you remember when that man tried to shoot Joe during a campaign rally in Escanaba, early in Joe's campaign?"

"Yes, and you took a bullet for Joe," she recalled, now gazing at the bullet wound scar in his lower abdomen.

"Well, when I was in the hospital, Jim took over for me as Joe's driver for his district campaign trips in the western U.P."

Velvet stared at him quizzically, wondering where his story was going.

"I don't know what happened; but after I recovered, I couldn't understand why Joe preferred Jim to accompany him on the district trips instead of me. Then I learned from a field staffer that Jim arranged nightly women companions for Joe when they were on district trips."

Velvet's jaw trembled as she absorbed the enormity of Taylor's revelation.

"I was told that Jim would attract young women at local bars after campaign events. After a few drinks, Jim would ask whether they would like to meet their congressman. When they agreed, he would take them to Joe's hotel room and then excuse himself for the evening, feigning fatigue from the long day."

Taylor paused, his voice drifting.

"It does not take much imagination to figure out what happened after Jim left," Taylor responded with a pained expression on his face.

She pushed Taylor away.

"You can't be serious," Velvet cried.

"I know. I didn't believe it either. But since Joe's death, I have heard substantially the same story from two others I trust. I had hoped and prayed that Jim would go away and with him the rumors of those sordid affairs. But when you said Jim would stay on the campaign, I knew I couldn't work with him ever again."

Velvet stared at him in disbelief.

How could this be true? Could Joe really have betrayed me?

But when she saw the innocence and pain in his eyes, she knew in her heart that he was being truthful.

Her face turned pale as she absorbed the true depths of Joe's betrayal.

She turned her gaze away from Taylor and towards the pool, trying to process what she had just heard.

Taylor's eyes now focused on the back of Velvet's black hair and trembling head.

A period of awkward silence followed, with neither being able to break the tension of the moment.

Then, the young woman who had accompanied Taylor to the pool interrupted the moment. She walked up to Taylor, brushing her hand across his neck and shoulders.

"Taylor, I am going to the locker room to get dressed and then go to the bar. Why don't you join me there after you finish talking with your friend?"

Velvet saw the embarrassed look on Taylor's face at the awkward moment.

"Taylor, I'm OK. Go with her?" Velvet replied softly.

Taylor had to decide whether to leave and break the tension or stay and continue their painful conversation. He paused, glancing at Velvet to test her sincerity. What more could he say? He reached for a nearby towel and appeared to follow the young woman to the locker room.

Her heartache at Joe's infidelity morphed into a blame mode. Why did Taylor not tell me this earlier, she wondered. Did everyone know except me? But then, after seeing his emotional outburst, she also realized how difficult it must have been for him to keep this infidelity a secret.

Though still struggling to recover from the initial shock of his revelation, she concluded that Taylor's decision to keep Joe's secret and not join her campaign was not an act of disloyalty but his way of protecting her from the pain of Joe's betrayal that she now felt.

Now she was watching someone walk away for whom she truly cared and needed to keep her political journey alive. And, she feared, he would be out of her life forever unless she spoke out.

"Taylor," she called out, "I need your help after I win the special election tomorrow. Joining my campaign is the most important thing you can do for me."

Taylor stopped and turned towards her. He dropped his towel and slouched down on the bench in front of the locker room. Then he looked up and forced the pained smile of someone for whom an enormous weight had just been lifted from his shoulders.

Maybe he will join me after all, she thought, though she was not sure in what capacity. The door to their relationship might still be ajar.

However, Taylor was thinking about something else.

He had not told her about the party's treachery. He did not have the heart to administer another body blow to her spirit. Maybe Jim was wrong, as he already had lied about Velvet's anger towards him. Or maybe she could overcome it, he rationalized. He had much more to contemplate before agreeing to rejoin the campaign.

Nodding to her, he stood up and walked into the locker room.

Velvet stared at the now empty locker room entrance for several minutes, wondering what Taylor's next move might be.

In a few minutes, Taylor emerged fully clothed, smiled, and waved at her as he walked out of the pool area. Rather than turn right to the bar where his female companion had beckoned, he instead walked straight to the elevator.

Velvet, still staggered by tales of Joe's infidelity, left the pool with a glimmer of hope for Taylor's return.

When she returned to her hotel room and checked her phone, she had a long string of texts from her staff and well-wishers. The voter turnout looked promising, and all predicted tomorrow would bring her a comfortable victory.

Velvet slept well, exhausted from the roller coaster events of the day. She left the casino hotel very early the next morning for the Soo to cast her ballot.

Election day arrived, and the race was called quickly in Velvet's favor. Within thirty minutes of the polls closing, the race was not even close. Velvet had drawn 51 percent of the vote, with the Republican drawing at 31 percent and Lorraine and the Green Party finishing third with a surprising 18 percent.

Congratulations poured in from her supporters. Barely one hour after the polls closed, Velvet announced to a fired-up crowd at the Soo Kewadin casino that her opponents had conceded, and she profusely thanked her supporters.

While Velvet was excited by her margin of victory, Democratic leaders were more impressed by Lorraine's strong showing as a progressive, third-party candidate in the conservative First District.

The press was quick to ask whether Velvet would enter the August Democratic primary and seek re-election in the fall. She deflected those questions as best she could, arguing she wanted to do something positive for the district in the few remaining months of the legislative session rather than gearing up for another campaign.

However, she left the door open by saying,

"I do not intend to run again unless I feel I can better serve my constituents by continuing to serve as their representative in Congress rather than as a citizen activist."

Word of her equivocation reached Lansing and prompted the Governor to place a personal telephone call to Velvet later that evening.

"Evangeline," the Governor began, "you know we have a deal on this reelection issue. You're not thinking about going back on your word, are you?"

Velvet assured him that her statement was that of any victorious candidate, and that she did not want to become an instant lame duck by announcing her intention not to seek re-election.

"Let me see if I can cut a deal to bring something positive to the district before I publicly reveal my plans," she argued.

"So, you will not run for re-election, right?" the Governor pressed.

"Governor, please let me enjoy this moment. The only thing I am certain about is that I want to do all I can in the few months ahead to help my district and my people. Re-election is the last thing I want to think about after this tough campaign."

The Governor seemed reassured, and after some casual pleasantries hung up.

Velvet was not about to tip her hand.

After learning of Joe's infidelity from Taylor, she learned firsthand the perils of blind trust in politics. I will not be played the fool again, she determined.

But she had a more immediate issue before her now that she had won; namely, how to handle the Jim Zenger issue.

She wanted Taylor back, that was certain. But Taylor refused to work with Jim. She felt she won her race because of Jim's expertise and needed him if she were successfully to run for re-election.

Maybe, since Taylor unburdened himself about Joe's infidelity and with further persuasion, he would soften his opposition to Jim.

And maybe Jim's role in Joe's infidelity was not as pernicious as staff members described to Taylor, though she would never look at Jim the same, no matter what the circumstances. She needed his expertise, not his friendship.

She summoned every ounce of her inner strength to suppress her pain in order to keep both men on her side. If I am going to run a successful campaign, I can't begin by cannibalizing my key staff members, she decided.

But in her heart, she knew the Zenger issue would not go away.

CHAPTER EIGHT

The Mining Miscalculation

"War has rules, mud wrestling has rules—politics has no rules."

—Ross Perot

WASHINGTON, D.C.
SPRING-SUMMER 2024

VELVET ARRIVED IN WASHINGTON WITH TWO ADVANTAGES MOST FRESH-
men do not enjoy: prior personal experience, as the spouse of a former
Congressman, and an experienced staff from the previous incumbent.

But her first days as an elected member of Congress on Capitol Hill
still were not happy ones. Gone was the "Mr. Smith Goes to Washington"
fascination with the edifices of Washington. While new members of Congress
were looking forward to social parties and galas, Velvet recalled her loneliness when she attended them with Joe.

Maybe my new political status will elevate me and my party will embrace me, she hoped.

She took the oath of office in a special early morning ceremony, but few members were present on the House floor. She proudly wore a colorful wraparound dress and her trademark green headband during the ceremony, but no one commented or even deigned to offer more than polite applause after she affirmed her oath.

Upon returning to her office, she huddled with her key staff members and expressed her frustration.

"There was hardly anyone there to watch me take the sacred oath of office," she complained. "And those who came all dressed in the same in bland suits and ties. Where's the cultural pride or heritage in this male-dominated, white society?" she asked.

Amy suggested that to bridge the Washington cultural and societal gap, she should begin by wearing more traditional women's clothing.

"Do you really think that would make a difference?" Velvet responded.

Others nodded in agreement.

Velvet frowned in disbelief.

"Well, I will try, but I won't give up my green headband!"

But the shunning by her colleagues continued, even as she bowed to the clothing advice of her staff. Except for a few western state members of Congress with First American constituencies, few bothered to converse with her, even during subway rides to the House floor for important votes.

The snubbing by members of both parties chipped away at her self-confidence. A lot like the racism I faced in my district, she observed, only this pettiness seemed more personal.

Rather than quietly accept the shunning, she decided to jump head-first into the political arena by introducing legislation like Joe did. Even if I serve only a few months, she thought, maybe I can accomplish something to make my political journey worthwhile. Joe made a big legislative splash in his first year, so why can't I?

However, Velvet's legislative initiatives as the newest member of Congress were limited not only by Congressional disinterest in her bills but also by the legislative calendar. When she arrived in mid-April, members were already scurrying back to their respective districts to prepare for their own November re-elections. The legislative calendar before November was short, an even greater barrier to her legislative priorities.

Undaunted, she directed her staff to draft legislation to fulfill her major campaign promises dealing with the environment and tribal casinos.

She sought advice for other legislative initiatives from Wenonah as well, but was advised to pick one key issue and one bill.

"Focus just on its passage during your short term in office and devote most of your time gathering cosponsors and seeking committee support for it."

Velvet shook her head in disagreement with her sister's advice.

"Don't fall into the freshman trap of introducing a flurry of bills with little or no support from congressional leadership or your fellow members of the Michigan delegation," Wenonah warned. "It does not end well."

"Thanks, Wenonah, but I want to pursue my own personal agenda. This year may be my only shot at following through on my campaign promises. Joe did it and, with the help of my ancestors, so will I," she responded.

Wenonah continued to counsel against her sister's shotgun approach, but Velvet would not hear of it.

"Sis, I know you are the political pro, but I need to do this my way this time."

The next week, she directed her staff to prepare bills to expand the Soo Locks, to fund clean-ups of mine waste in Copper Country, to decrease federal oversight of Native American casinos, and to establish wilderness designation for parts of the national forest lands in the U.P.

She sent around "Dear Colleague" letters to members of her Michigan delegation prior to introducing the bills, asking for co-sponsors. Undeterred when no Michigan Congressional office responded to her request, she plowed forward anyway.

When she finally was allotted five minutes to speak on the House floor, she marched in before a nearly empty house chamber to announce the introduction of her four bills, attaching a prepared statement for each one to be printed in the Congressional Record.

Amy issued press releases for the bills after their introduction, and Velvet anxiously awaited public reaction to them.

Soon, Velvet began receiving letters from constituents asking about the status of her bills. She called a staff meeting to discuss their legislative progress. Her staff reported the bills were received, given bill numbers, and sent to the appropriate committees. But no committee action was scheduled.

"So, when will I be testifying about my bills?" she asked.

Her staff shrugged and looked at Tom for guidance.

Tom, her legislative director and a holdover from Joe's staff, delivered her another sobering lesson in her political education. As a member of the minority Democratic Party in the House, she had little power to do anything more to move her bills. House Republicans were not about to help the woman who won their First District seat.

"So, you are saying they are all dead in the water?" she exclaimed.

"Well, not dead, but on life support unless something dramatic makes any of your bills relevant to the political agenda of the Republican leadership," he responded.

"Damn," she said under her breath.

She was further weakened by being placed on two committees with little political power to affect the success of her bills: the Ethics and Science and Technology committees.

"Can I highlight my bills by barnstorming the district to show I am keeping my campaign promises?" Velvet asked.

Her new administrative assistant delivered the bad news on the travel front. Her office staff budget was almost exhausted, as Joe had hired more staffers and interns than was sustainable for supporting five district offices. Joe also had exhausted most of the district travel and postage budget, so there were no office funds to tap. She couldn't afford to take the weekly trips back to the district that had made Joe so popular.

And her fear of flying over Gitche Gumee after the dreadful toll it had taken on her family meant private flights offered by her supporters to remote parts of the western U.P. were also out, further limiting her exposure to constituents in regions where she was not well known.

Her constituents were not happy with their invisible representative, and she received many calls, emails, and letters criticizing her for not attending meetings or popular local events that Joe had attended.

Recognizing her precarious political position, some staffers urged her to use her constituency service power. Earning the gratitude of individual constituents who were beneficiaries of her personal intervention with federal agencies would be useful for her re-election campaign.

But Velvet wanted big legislative achievements to show her detractors that she was up to the task like Joe, so she instead delegated these services to her caseworkers.

Jim Zenger suggested a slightly different route, arguing she should focus on an issue that would appeal to business interests and environmental interests alike to garner broad political support. He argued that identifying an important local issue under the purview of a federal agency and using personal intervention rather than legislation would be a faster route for headline results.

Velvet liked the concept but was wary of Jim and his alleged role in procuring sex for Joe. There would be a reckoning for him, but now was not the time. She still needed his contacts and expertise, she rationalized, but refused to put the fate of my campaign in his hands.

Failing to heed the advice of her sister, her staff, or Jim, Velvet put all her energy into pushing all four of her bills simultaneously, hoping that at least one of them might trigger legislative action. But her calls, letters, and personal pleas for support—even from her Michigan colleagues—went unanswered.

After several more weeks of committee inactivity on her bills, she called the few Congressional colleagues who still conversed with her and asked for their advice on moving her bills. Three Democratic Congresswomen met in her office and delivered the bad news. The Republican committee chairs had no intention of even holding hearings on her bills.

They further disclosed that they had heard rumors that the Michigan Democratic party leadership was already vetting candidates to run against her in the August primary, only a couple of months away.

The latter disclosure floored her.

"I'm barely seated and already the knives are out! My own party is plotting against me!" she cried to her colleagues.

After they left, she sat alone in her office searching for a solution to her predicament. She would not go down without a fight.

I am going to win this seat again and prove my detractors wrong, she concluded.

She now was running not just for her district, but for personal vindication as well.

To get there, she needed a new strategy to get re-elected. Her legislative strategy was a flop. Begrudgingly, she called Jim and asked him to elaborate on his regulatory strategy. It seemed a better fallback approach than the other, less glamorous individual constituent service option.

"It's pretty simple," he explained. "Pick an issue that's important to your district, propose a solution that will not upset the major interest groups concerned about the issue, and find a friendly regulatory agency to implement your proposal with no Congressional action."

"That sounds impossible. How can I come up with a solution that won't upset someone?" Velvet responded.

"Well, first pick an issue that really bothers you," he began.

"Mining pollution," she replied.

"OK," he continued, "so attack the problem by regulating future mining activity rather than current mining operations."

"So, I wouldn't be fighting existing companies, but only potential new ones. How does this accomplish anything?"

"It's a symbolic act but one that you can win without a Congressional vote and that can provide you with an accomplishment in the few months you have before the August primary."

"But I want to accomplish something meaningful."

"This is just to get something done now so you can do something more meaningful after you are re-elected," Jim assured her.

I don't like him, nor do I trust him, but this is about politics and not personality, she concluded. He's the expert Joe relied on and what he says makes political sense, given my limited options.

But I am going to handle this from this point on, she decided.

She asked her staff to gather information on mining pollution incidents that had occurred over the past five years in her district. Using that information to paint a picture of growing mining pollution in the district, she would seek regulatory help through both the Department of Interior and the EPA.

Tom composed a letter for her to the Secretary of the Department of Interior in mid-June, asking him to suspend issuing any new permits for mineral extraction in the U.P. on federal lands until the department held public hearings. Amy had copies of the letter sent to the local press outlets for circulation. Velvet also asked that the Secretary hold an immediate public hearing to get the local public comment on the future of mining in the Western Upper Peninsula.

Next, she had Tom draft a letter to the EPA Region V Administrator, requesting the EPA hold local hearings in her district to identify any public health effects that mining pollution may have had on the local population. This additional step she felt would strengthen her permit moratorium proposal to stop future harm.

Velvet assumed her requests would appeal to environmentalists who opposed more mining and current mining operators who did not want more mining competition in the region. Jim argued that her appearance at the public hearings would be an excellent forum to increase her visibility and project the image of a doer and a protector of local interests.

Amy and Tom both strongly disagreed with Jim's idea.

"Velvet", Tom argued, "why would a Republican Administration want to help you?"

Amy agreed with Tom.

"If any of you have better idea, let's hear it," Velvet replied.

Both Amy and Tom continued to argue the plan would not work and might blow up in her face if the Administration refused to act. But they couldn't offer an appealing concrete alternative.

"Well, it's the only plan on the table, so please let's work together on this," Velvet instructed.

It was not long after the public release of her agency correspondence that her plan met unexpected resistance from the very parties she sought to please.

Local environmentalists wanted a total ban on new mining permits, not a mere pause. They argued a pause would undercut their current efforts to impose a permanent ban and were more concerned about current mining activity than speculative future mining.

Meanwhile, after further research, Tom discovered that several current mining operators were the primary applicants for new permits and were unhappy with her permit moratorium effort. They were also worried about the adverse publicity that would result from EPA public health hearings, perhaps triggering lawsuits by citizens alleging health effects from existing mining activities.

On July 10, the Secretary of the Interior Department sent a letter rejecting her request for a permit moratorium, characterizing it as "impractical and shortsighted" for the mining interests in the area.

But on the same day, the regional EPA agreed to hold a health-focused public hearing in Marquette on July 22, giving Velvet a glimmer of hope that her plan might still bear positive fruit.

* * *

Velvet was excited about the EPA hearing and arrived a day early in Marquette to prepare. There was a sizeable crowd when she appeared at the

Marquette city council chamber room the next morning. She saw members of the local press there and was hopeful for some positive press coverage.

Velvet kicked off the hearing by delivering an opening statement, explaining the importance of the hearing and her gratitude to the EPA for holding it.

But the hearing quickly transformed from a forum for Velvet to burnish her image to a cauldron of anger. One by one, environmental and mining interest speakers vented their displeasure with Velvet's moratorium proposal and its ineffectiveness in addressing health concerns, the supposed focus of the EPA hearing. She sat at the meeting speechless, as they characterized her as an opportunist who had not lifted a finger in Congress to address real public health concerns.

The media coverage was devastating. Even some members of Michigan's Congressional delegation criticized her efforts in news articles, describing her efforts as weak and opportunistic.

Rather than bolstering her campaign for re-election, the hearing only emboldened calls by both political parties to defeat Velvet.

With Congress in recess and her mining permit gambit in tatters, Velvet knew she would face a strong primary challenge for her party's nomination in the August primary, with no coherent message to rally her supporters. Though she had been in office only three short months, there was no honeymoon period or post-election afterglow to fall back upon.

Anger by environmentalists and mining businesses alike replaced the goodwill towards a widow taking her husband's seat. Her failure accelerated criticism that she had neither Joe's skill nor passion for legislating. There also was growing discontent by her constituents for her invisibility in the district since her election.

Student and tribal support were barely holding for Velvet. But there was not much else. And to add insult to injury, her likely general election Republican challenger was the same man Joe defeated to win the seat.

Early campaign ads by her likely Republican opponent ended with the slogan: "We need an iron fist in Washington, not a Velvet glove."

However, the most surprising political development was the emergence of her newest primary opponent, none other than Lorraine Sampson. Lorraine had done so well as the Green Party candidate in the April special election that Democratic party leaders and officials across the board recruited her to run for Velvet's seat.

Many pollsters declared Velvet's campaign to retain her seat over, and some of her staffers migrated to more secure jobs either in other races or in the private sector. Her biggest loss was her administrative assistant, who left to become Lorraine's campaign manager after only two months on the job.

Amy stayed, assuming the role of acting administrative assistant, and the campaign continued its bumpy ride towards the August primary. But Amy struggled to keep the campaign and office operations on a steady keel, as fundraising was not her strength and many major Democratic donors already had jumped to Lorraine. Only strong tribal financial support gave her some breathing room.

It soon became clear that Lorraine also had co-opted the Democratic field of key environmental leaders and Democratic-friendly business interests, leaving Velvet at a decided disadvantage despite her incumbency advantage.

With the primary election just a few weeks away and legislative prospects dead in the water, Velvet concluded Jim was no longer the political asset Joe had once extolled. She remembered her sister's advice to listen to those she trusted, and she trusted and needed Taylor, not Jim.

She called Jim, who had left Washington after the mining plan failure to organize a grassroots operation in Escanaba.

"Jim, I really appreciate all you have done for me, but I have to make some changes. I am going to ask Taylor to join the campaign and run the field operations."

"What?" Jim snorted. "What does he know about field operations?"

"Taylor has been doing some solid work on the campuses, and I think he might give us a fresh approach in the waning weeks," she replied.

"You are dead politically if you do this, and I will quit," Jim threatened.

"Well, that is certainly your choice, and I will make sure we fairly compensate you."

"Look Congresswoman, you've made some poor political decisions, but this is your worst. You need me, not Taylor."

"I have made up my mind. Thank you for your service, but I'm going to take a new path forward in these last few weeks. Sorry you will not be with us."

"Good luck with your lover boy," Jim scoffed, breaking off the call.

Lover boy? she laughed to herself. Well, at least that unpleasant call is over.

But now she recognized her next step was even more important and uncertain.

She swallowed hard and called Taylor.

"Taylor," Velvet asked delicately, "Jim is gone, and I need your help in the few weeks remaining before the August Democratic primary. Will you join me?"

Sensing both the urgent need to help Velvet and repulsed by the blatant efforts of her party to replace her with Lorraine, Taylor was ready to commit.

The only impediment had been Jim, and now he was gone.

"Velvet, I am with you to the end," he replied.

CHAPTER NINE

The Cover-up?

"It is almost always the cover-up rather than the event that causes trouble."

—Former U.S. Senator Howard Baker

MARQUETTE, MICHIGAN
JULY 2024

WITH THE AUGUST PRIMARY DATE LOOMING, A SEEMINGLY UNRELATED event occurred earlier in the year which would further scramble the First Congressional District race.

A rare earthquake shook the central region of Lake Superior, causing it to spew from its bowels tons of long-lost debris.

The tremors triggered fears among environmentalists that the aftershocks also might stir the Lake Michigan and Lake Huron lakebeds, causing another Line 5 pipeline rupture. Though no significant vibrations rippled south from Lake Superior, it was a reminder of the potential danger the underwater pipeline posed to the Great Lakes.

Several days after the quake in late February, large objects began washing up along the southern shores of Lake Superior, including the beach area around the Upper Peninsula's most populous city, Marquette. The largest objects, ranging from old logs to remnants from sunken ships, lodged in shallow areas along the shoreline, forming a wall-like barrier between the city's beach and the deep waters of the Big Lake.

Shoreline property owners found the debris not only unsightly but also potentially dangerous to boaters and waders brave enough to endure Lake Superior's icy cold water. Private estimates of debris clean-up and disposal were in the millions of dollars, more than local property associations were willing to pay.

After unsuccessful efforts to get funding from cash-strapped local units of government, a wealthy shoreline owners' association wrote to Velvet in May after the ice along the shoreline had receded, asking for federal aid.

Velvet's staff flagged the issue for her personal attention. But at that time Velvet was not particularly concerned about the needs of a group of wealthy shoreline owners. Another rich white person issue, she thought, and handed it off to one of her junior staff members to "look into it" with no specific guidance or sense of urgency.

Without her personal engagement, the issue languished in her office files while Velvet pursued first her legislative strategy and then her ill-fated mining regulatory one. It was only with the August primary looming that the shoreline debris issue resurfaced during a staff meeting, hastily called to save her sinking primary campaign.

"OK, put your heads together folks," Velvet pleaded over the din of staff chattering. "What can we do to turn these bad mining headlines around? Is there an issue out there we are missing?"

A junior staffer raised the Marquette debris problem, showing her recent local newspaper headlines calling on the President to help fund the clean-up.

116

"Why aren't they working with us rather than the White House?" Velvet asked. "Didn't I ask someone to handle this issue?" she asked the staffer.

Tom, her legislative assistant, jumped in.

"Velvet, it's going to take your personal intervention to get the Administration to pay any attention to this local issue."

Velvet's face dropped.

"Well, I am jumping in right now. Everyone else, please search your files for other issues while I look into this," she instructed, dismissing everyone except the junior staffer, Amy, and Tom.

After being briefed on the debris issue and hearing estimates for remediation, Velvet turned to Tom.

"Tom, is there a federal program that might fund the clean-up?"

"Well, what first comes to mind is a FEMA disaster declaration," Tom replied.

"Draft me a one-page memo about what I need to know about FEMA. Drop everything you are doing and get it to me today. I want to call the White House ASAP and get the ball rolling. Amy, I want you to prepare a draft press release for the local papers showing we are on top of this issue."

Within the hour, Tom drafted a memo outlining the applicable provisions of the Federal Emergency Management Act and met with Velvet to go over any questions she might have.

Velvet skimmed through Tom's memo and smiled.

"So, I pretty much just have to describe the nature of the disaster and ask the President to declare it a national emergency in order to get FEMA aid?" Velvet asked.

"The request has to be made by the Governor, not you, but you can begin the process by coordinating with him."

"I don't think the Governor is going to do me any favors now," Velvet sighed, "but I'll call him, anyway. Anything else?"

"Well, there is a lot of data gathering and paperwork we need to do, but the important thing is to get the President to agree to such a declaration.

It's his call, and the process begins with coordinating with the Governor to bring it to his attention," Tom explained.

Armed with this information and with Tom and Amy listening, Velvet placed a call to the Governor. The Governor's chief of staff took her call; and, after listening to her plea for working together on this issue, explained they had already explored this option with the White House.

"We were told it was unlikely to justify a Presidential declaration," the chief of staff concluded.

"What if I called the President?" she asked. "Would the Governor apply if I got a green light from the White House? After all, it's not a political issue to help needy people."

"Congresswoman, we appreciate your concern, but the Governor has strong ties with the President as a fellow Republican. If he could not move the White House, I'm not sure your intervention would be any more successful. But, by all means, try if you think it will work," the chief of staff replied.

"I will," Velvet resolved. "Stay tuned."

Velvet called the White House, telling the operator her call was urgent. An assistant to the White House Chief of Staff took her call. Velvet explained she needed the President to declare the Lake Superior shoreline a natural disaster area in order to activate the full resources of FEMA.

"Is that the urgent issue you're calling about?" he responded. "Didn't this debris issue happen months ago?"

It surprised Velvet that a lower-level staff member even knew about the incident, but she continued to press the issue.

"It wasn't an emergency until all the ice melted, as the debris couldn't be removed until then. But now, in mid-summer, it has become a real safety threat," Velvet replied.

"The President is very busy right now, but I will forward your request to my boss, and we will get back to you as soon as we can," he replied. "Thank you for calling."

"That didn't sound very hopeful," Velvet frowned after the call ended.

"Well, you have taken the first step and have shown you are taking the initiative," Tom replied. "Shows your constituents you are trying to help."

Amy suggested they issue a press release headlined: "Representative LeBlanc calls on the White House to declare Marquette shoreline a disaster area."

"OK, but I want to have something happen rather than just sit here and wait for the White House to respond," she protested.

Tom suggested she call the Congressional liaison for the Coast Guard while waiting for a White House response. She agreed and made the call, but was advised that it was not something the Coast Guard could fund without White House approval.

The next day, she called the White House again, but was told her FEMA request was still pending before the President, and he had made no decision.

Three days later, she finally received a call from a White House aide on behalf of the White House Chief of Staff informing her that the President had denied her request for FEMA financial assistance. The White House would issue a statement later that day on that issue and several other disaster requests.

That afternoon, the White House issued its promised press release, announcing several disaster requests that were approved and several denied. A sentence at the end of the release mentioned the Marquette situation, pointing out that Representative LeBlanc had sought disaster relief but "her intervention was not actionable since it did not follow the standard protocol."

That sentence stung Velvet.

"What a dirty political trick to put that sentence in the press release!" Velvet gasped. "So unnecessary."

"They play for keeps during an election year, Velvet. It's clear we can expect no favors from either the Governor or the White House," Tom advised.

When word of her failure became public through the White House press release, candidates from both major parties pounced again on her ineffectiveness, promising positive action if they assumed her office in January.

Lorraine Sampson, Velvet's chief Democratic primary challenger, went one step further. Scoffing at Velvet's ineffective efforts, she announced she soon would release a private sector solution to the shoreline debris problem. Lorraine was in a unique position to fulfill her promise, as she had become the paid spokesperson for a major Marquette land development project dubbed Gitche Gumee Estates. Her job was to promote the environmentally responsible development of the project along the Marquette shoreline.

The Gitche Gumee Estates developers, headed by two wealthy business owners, hired Lorraine in 2022 to enhance the "green" image of their project. Their project involved the development of high-rise condos, green spaces, and golf courses along several miles of Lake Superior shoreline west of the city of Marquette.

Though they previously had been major campaign contributors to Joe's campaign, they were now making huge independent campaign expenditures on behalf of Lorraine, who had become the chief Democratic challenger to Velvet in the August 2024 primary.

On August 1, at a press conference held in Marquette, Lorraine unveiled the Gitche Gumee Estates "Protect by the Pound" plan. Under this plan, the developers would pay university students to remove debris along the three-mile coastline where the development owned property. The developers provided Northern Michigan University (NMU) student organizations with numbered and colored tags. The students were to remove foreign objects weighing at least one pound, tag the objects, transport the tagged debris to designated pickup areas on the beach, and send pictures of the tagged debris to the developers for credit.

Each week, the developers would send trucks to pick up and dispose of the debris, weigh each tagged object, and credit the student organization with 10 cents for every pound of solid debris removed.

The NMU students enthusiastically embraced the "Protect by the Pound" program, garnering tremendous positive media coverage not only for the developers but also for Lorraine's campaign. Praised as an excellent example of a private, civic-minded effort to address the shoreline debris issue, it further highlighted the ineffectiveness of Velvet as a member of Congress.

Over 100 NMU students representing a dozen student organizations began a frenzied effort to pull waterlogged timber from past lumbering days and shipwrecks, cargo boxes, and even some old cars parts and other illegally dumped equipment. After only four days of operation in early August, students had pulled almost 30 tons of debris from the Marquette shoreline. Local newspapers featured Lorraine on their front pages, presenting checks to student leaders totaling $60,000.

Local news headlines praised the "Protect by the Pound" success, putting Velvet's struggling campaign on defense as social media posts and letters to the editor in local news outlets poured in, criticizing her inaction.

* * *

Scrambling to fend off negative local press coverage, Velvet left Washington and returned to her home in Christmas, where she would be headquartered for the last weeks of her primary campaign. It was there that she received a very troubling letter.

The letter was from an NMU student named Jamal Jones. He described serious illnesses suffered by several students after handling three 55-gallon steel drums they had dragged ashore during the "Protect by the Pound" campaign. He explained the developers would only pay for solid waste from the lake, so the students punctured the three heavy barrels, causing what they thought was rusty lake water to pour onto the beach.

Since the drums were thick, the students had to use spikes and sledgehammers to puncture the barrels, causing the contents to spray the five students. The liquid released emitted a pungent odor, and shortly after exposure, the five students experienced nausea, nosebleeds, and vomiting. One student fainted, and an ambulance was called to take all five students to the nearby hospital in Marquette.

Then came the most chilling paragraph in Jamal's letter:

"The hospital emergency room doctors initially diagnosed the students' conditions as a flu-like virus, but the suddenness of the illness among all five students suggested possible exposure to a toxic or perhaps even a radioactive substance."

"A radioactive substance?" Velvet exclaimed aloud.

The term "radioactive" reminded Velvet of a dumping mystery decades ago.

Historically, the Great Lakes had experienced a poor environmental relationship with the federal government, which had frequently used Lake Superior as a military-waste dumping ground. Out of sight, out of mind, was the apparent rationale.

One particular incident came to mind concerning the decision by the U.S. Army Corps of Engineers to dump barrels of munition waste into Lake Superior between 1959 and 1962. The official position of the Corps was that the dumping was limited to the western end of the lake and only involved harmless munition waste sealed in barrels.

Later exploration of one of the official dumping sites near Duluth, Minnesota, by a local environmental group recovered barrels containing toxic chemicals mixed with ammunition waste. The Corps denied the charge after seizing the barrels.

She also remembered reading about a private submarine explorer who had scanned another official Lake Superior dumpsite and found detectable levels of radiation. The Corps emphatically disputed this claim as well.

I assumed those were just rumors, she thought to herself. But what if they were true?

The Corps' credibility on barrel dumping was further tarnished by a more recent university research report alleging that the Corps had grossly underestimated the scope of the prior dumping. Rather than the dumping of a few hundred barrels at seven dump sites, as initially reported by the Corps, the report concluded the dumping was closer to 1500 barrels at over fifteen sites.

Her hands shook as I reread the letter, shocked by its potential environmental implications.

Could there be a connection between the barrels found on the Marquette beach—which were unmarked except for a few small numbers embossed on the sides—and the barrels dumped by the Corps more than a half century ago?

Velvet called a local physician she trusted. After describing the students' symptoms, she posed the pivotal question: "Would conventional munition waste cause the symptoms the students experienced, or would toxic or even radioactive waste be the more likely culprit?"

The doctor replied guardedly, "I know of no known conventional munition waste that would cause such symptoms."

"Could toxic or radioactive waste cause such symptoms?" she repeated.

"Those symptoms would be consistent with such exposure, yes," he replied.

She thanked the doctor and hung up.

I must talk to the student who wrote the letter, she thought.

She called the student, who had provided his cell phone number in his letter.

"Jamal, this is Congresswoman LeBlanc. I am responding to your letter about the student illness issue you raised. If I come to your campus today, can we talk?"

Jamal stammered, "Of course!"

"I'll be there early this afternoon," Velvet replied and, after arranging a meeting place at the Student Union, called her field office in the Soo.

"Please find someone to drive to my house and pick me up. I have to be in Marquette this afternoon."

After being assured a car was on its way, she made one more call.

I have never needed Taylor more than I do right now, she thought. With that, she called him and told him to drop everything and fly to Marquette.

"Is time of the essence on this issue?" Taylor asked, as he was busy with student voter-mobilization efforts.

"It is, Taylor, or I would not ask you to come now."

"I'm on my way," Taylor confirmed.

* * *

When her driver arrived at Christmas, Velvet jumped in the car, and they sped towards Marquette.

Foremost on her mind during the trip was how much she missed having Taylor as her driver. Taylor's calm and easy presence would have been welcomed during her tough re-election campaign. Even more so to prepare me for meetings like this, she thought wistfully.

But these were the cards she was holding. Taylor was valiantly trying to hold together her fragile coalition of environmental students, dispirited by Velvet's ineffectiveness and not inclined to take an active part in her general election campaign.

But she needed him with her now. His organizational work would have to wait.

During her drive to Marquette, Velvet pondered how to frame her conversation with Jamal, hoping her sudden visit to NMU would not tip her hand as to her fears of what might have caused these student illnesses.

Jamal was a junior, majoring in environmental studies and was the president of an NMU student recycling organization. His home was Chicago, but he found the natural beauty of the Marquette area to be irresistible and was the only member of his high school class to venture so far north.

Arriving on the NMU campus, she spotted Jamal sitting on a bench at the Student Union. Jamal was a young black male and easy to recognize among the few students milling around this overwhelmingly white community, as the fall semester had not yet begun.

Velvet motioned to her driver to pull the campaign car up to the curb and emerged from the car to greet Jamal. After exchanging pleasantries, she invited him to join her, and they motored to a local restaurant he had recommended.

Seated at the restaurant, Velvet inquired about the health of the five hospitalized students. Jamal told her that four were still hospitalized and one had been released, though she was still weak and unlikely to attend the first week of fall classes. The other four suffered recurrent nosebleeds, weight loss, and two had lost most of their hair.

He described how healthy his classmates had been prior to their exposure to the barrel contents, and the financial support that the Gitche Gumee Estates developers had provided to take care of all their health costs.

"Can you take me to where the barrels are?" Velvet asked.

"No, the barrels were removed as soon as the ambulance took the students away. Someone—I think the developers—also sent a team of workers to remove a large area of sand where the barrel contents had spilled."

Velvet now realized that not only did she suspect a dangerous contamination incident, but so did the developers.

"Can you show me the site where they found the barrels?" she inquired.

Jamal nodded and showed her a picture of the disposal site on his cell phone, as pictures of the collected debris were required to receive financial credit for their work. The background vegetation in the picture made it relatively easy to locate the site.

"I have the rest of the day free, so I'll be happy to guide you there," Jamal responded.

"Please forward that picture to me so I can look more closely at the barrels," Velvet asked.

"Done," Jamal replied.

With that, she called a good friend from her early environmental activism days, an NMU chemistry professor by the name of Dr. Charles Holli.

"Chuck, this is Velvet. I'm here on campus and need you to come with me and bring whatever sampling tools you need. I have a possible environmental contamination issue and I need your expert opinion. Can you help me? I can be at your office in ten minutes to pick you up."

"OK, Velvet. I assume this is big, so I will cancel my appointments and meet you at the Student Union. But give me thirty minutes, OK?"

"OK, Chuck. I owe you."

"Joe got us some big-time money for research, so this is the least I can do to pay you both back," Holli responded.

Joe's legislative accomplishments paid some important, unexpected political dividends, Velvet thought.

After ending the call, she turned to Jamal, who by now was visibly shaken by the serious nature of the conversation he had just overheard.

"Jamal, I need you to keep everything you hear on this visit confidential. This may be nothing or it may be a significant pollution spill, but we must keep it under wraps until we know what we're dealing with. I don't want to cause a panic."

Jamal again nodded but became increasingly uncomfortable. Unbeknownst to Velvet, he too had experienced some of the same symptoms as his fellow students only in a milder form, as his exposure had been to the ill students and not the actual barrel contents. But he also wanted to figure out this puzzle.

Velvet's car soon pulled up to the science building, where they scooped up Dr. Holli.

Just then, Taylor called. Recognizing the urgency of Velvet's request, he had asked a student pilot he knew to fly him to Marquette.

"I just landed in Marquette."

"We're on our way to get you," Velvet replied and directed her driver to the airport.

Taylor was standing outside the small terminal when Velvet's car arrived.

Once in the car, she introduced him to Jamal and Dr. Holli. She then explained the situation to Taylor and her fears of a major environmental spill as they motored together to the beach.

When they arrived at the shoreline, Jamal guided them to the site where the barrels had been punctured. However, both the barrels and the rust-colored sand were gone and replaced by a fresh quantity of clean sand. To the untrained eye, nothing seemed out of place.

"Is there anything left you can sample from the beach?" Taylor asked.

"Yes, since sand is a poor medium for containing liquids," Dr. Holli responded.

He began taking samples of the sand on the perimeter of the excavation site, noting the boundaries between the newly deposited sand and the existing sand and vegetation. After he had collected enough samples, they returned to the car and headed back to NMU.

While the conversation focused upon Dr. Holli's forthcoming analysis, Velvet didn't disclose her suspicion of a cover-up by the developers or the Corps of Engineers. Not yet, she thought. I need to hear an unvarnished analysis of the sand first.

Velvet thanked both Jamal and Dr. Holli for their help, and, after dropping them off along with her staff driver in Marquette, Taylor took over and drove her back home to Christmas.

On their ride home, Velvet weighed whether to disclose to Taylor her true suspicions and their implications for Lorraine's candidacy. She had a nagging concern—am I doing this because I want to find a scandal and a cover-up to enhance my re-election prospects, or am I truly just concerned about a major environmental incident in Lake Superior?

I suppose it is both, but that's OK if the result is protecting Gitche Gumee, she assured herself.

While awaiting Dr. Holli's analysis, her thoughts turned to the other questions.

Where were the barrels?

Where was the contaminated soil?

What company excavated the site and who hired them?

Since this was such a sensitive list of questions, she sought the answers from a person who had a student's perspective, an acute environmental sensitivity, and a fair attitude to help her find the answers.

Clearly, I am looking at that very person, she thought, staring at Taylor.

She asked Taylor to stay for a minute when their car pulled up to her house in Christmas and parked. "Taylor, I have a few questions. If I lose the primary, should I stay in politics or return to Christmas?"

Taylor warned of the tough politics ahead should she continue, but he thought the contamination issue was a potential crisis that she could best address by making it part of the 2020 general election campaign.

"You should continue to investigate the barrel issue if Dr. Holli's soil analysis confirms a major environmental spill."

Velvet smiled.

"This is a potentially huge issue; one that will require investigations beyond your current term in office. But you could start the ball rolling as a sitting member of Congress."

Velvet then revealed her suspicions about radioactivity as the source of the student illnesses in Marquette. Taylor was stone-faced.

"I think Gitche Gumee may have unlocked a dirty secret that the Corps has kept from us for decades," Velvet responded solemnly.

Then Velvet posed her most troubling request: "Would you help me get information about the spill from the developers?"

She knew he could gather this information through his past association with Lorraine, and that he still had many friends working on Lorraine's campaign that he could tap. She also knew that such information could upend Lorraine's election bid.

Taylor's eyes dropped to the floor, avoiding eye contact with Velvet. It truly was a painful request. He was being asked to use his personal contacts with friends in Lorraine's camp to undermine their candidate.

An uncomfortable period of silence ensued.

"I know this is unfair of me to ask, but it is so important, and I don't know where else to get this information," Velvet pleaded.

This was the part of political campaigning she despised—using friends for political gain. But she also realized the extraordinary environmental threat that this situation posed if the barrels were indeed what she suspected and she did nothing to stop it.

"Are you asking me to do this for personal reasons or political ones?" he asked, echoing a similar question he had posed to Joe years ago.

"Both," she replied candidly.

He nodded and replied, "I'll look into it."

Velvet nodded, stepped out of the car, and he sped off.

* * *

Velvet sat by her phone, waiting for Holli's analysis of the soil samples. She fell asleep on her couch, only to be awakened by the loud ringing of the call she expected but also dreaded.

"Velvet, this is Chuck. I examined the soil samples, and they were not good. The samples reflect a virtual cauldron of toxic chemicals—and some low levels of radioactive waste. This is not munitions-related but the highest levels of some known human carcinogens I have ever examined, and these were just the diluted samples taken from the periphery of the spill. Bad news."

A very uncomfortable pause occurred before Velvet responded.

"Are you sure about this, Chuck?"

"I'm afraid I am," he replied.

"OK, text me your findings and I will be back in touch. I may need to talk to you again about this soon," she replied, and hung up.

Her mind flitted between the horror of the spill and the possibility that more such barrels might still be out there. Was this a massive government cover-up and, if so, who was responsible?

She then shifted to a more immediate political question: where were the barrels and why had the Gitche Gumee Estates developers and Lorraine not released any information about them?

She tried calling Taylor repeatedly, but he was not picking up his phone. So, she called Amy and asked her to check the logs of all waste disposal sites in the Marquette area to see if Gitche Gumee Estates had deposited any solid waste in the past month.

Pulling out all stops, Velvet called her cousin Frank, who had become chair of the Sault tribe, and asked if he knew of any friendly state or federal environmental officials whom she could contact. He gave her the names and contact numbers of several at the EPA and the Michigan Department of Environmental Quality, the MDEQ.

"I will personally make the calls and explain the importance of this issue," Velvet promised.

Amy asked how quickly she needed the information.

"This may be something big, but I can't explain it to you right now. Just make this your top priority," Velvet urged.

It wasn't until midmorning of the next day that she heard from Amy. She had collected the waste disposal site information within a fifty-mile radius of Marquette, and had an intern review the online logs to see who recently had used the facilities.

"We found no written record of anyone associated with Gitche Gumee Estates or the developers," Amy concluded.

So, where do I go now? How can I find the waste from the beach clean-up operation, she asked herself?

She called Taylor again and left another message. Did he have any information to share?

A few minutes later, her phone rang, and she got her answer.

Taylor found little information about the incident from Lorraine's staff, and Lorraine offered no additional information when he met with her and viewed the development on a brief driving tour. Similar calls to friends Taylor knew from Lorraine's earlier campaign also provided no clues.

Velvet was deflated and did not respond.

"However, I talked to a local reporter who covered the debris clean-up and had taken photos at the site, including pictures of the clean-up crew who removed the contaminated sand."

"And?"

"I recognized one of the crew members as a former member of Lorraine's Green Party campaign staff. I tracked him down and found he was hospitalized with the same symptoms as the students on the beach—nausea, vomiting, and nosebleeds. When I tried to contact him at home where he was recovering, he refused to talk."

"What?" Velvet exclaimed.

"It gets worse," Taylor continued.

"I got a call about an hour later from Lorraine's campaign manager—your former AA—telling me to stop contacting Lorraine and her campaign staff. He then issued a thinly veiled threat to drop the issue or 'face some serious consequences.'"

Velvet did not respond, and an uncomfortable silence ensued.

"I did some more research and found the trucking company contracted by the developers to remove the debris from the beach. The developers hired three of their employees."

"Go on," Velvet implored.

"I got a copy of an email sent by the developers to those employees with instructions to 'promptly dispose of all beach debris in a low-lying area of the real estate development,'" he reported.

"That would explain why we couldn't find any record of waste deposits by the Gitche Gumee Estates at the public disposal sites," Velvet replied triumphantly.

There was a pause and then Taylor declared, "I think the barrels and soil are buried somewhere in the Gitche Gumee Estates development."

"Taylor," Velvet began as she swallowed hard, "can you forward this information to Amy and me? I think we have a problem on an immense scale, and we'll have to move on this quickly if we are going to find those barrels."

Taylor agreed.

Now she had a decision to make. Should she alert the press about this information before she had conclusive evidence to support a cover-up? And should she inject Lorraine into the investigation so close to the mid-August primary?

After consulting with Amy and Wenonah, she determined it was now or never. If she waited until after the primary and lost, she would lose any leverage she might have with federal agencies and Lorraine.

The environment was on the line, and she was going to act. To return to the village of Christmas and sing environmental protest songs was not the path to protecting the Upper Peninsula she loved and the waters of Gitche Gumee.

"Taylor, I think this issue is the whole ball game, so let's do this right!" Velvet exclaimed.

She arranged a conference call with Amy and her acting press secretary, Angela, in Washington. She described her suspicions and her proposed plans for the last days of the campaign. Then she asked Amy to arrange an interview for her with a friendly reporter from the *Marquette Mining Journal* to announce her findings.

The next day in her press interview, Velvet provided the reporter with Dr. Holli's chemical analysis and the Gitche Gumee Estates email, resulting in newspaper headlines that raised a public outcry for an EPA investigation.

Velvet directed Angela to release her letter to the EPA that Taylor had drafted, demanding that the EPA investigate the whereabouts of the barrels and the tainted soil, supplying the EPA with the fruits of their previous research. She also wrote to the Corps and the Gitche Gumee Estates developers demanding the release of the missing barrels.

The EPA was reluctant to investigate since it was so close to the August primary. However, public pressure and Velvet's public demands in letters to the EPA and Corps of Engineers forced them to act, and they requested permission to inspect the designated debris dumping area on the Gitche Gumee Estates.

Lorraine, as a spokesperson for the developers, decried Velvet's claims as a politically motivated witch hunt, and as an irresponsible allegation that hurt both the development and the Marquette community.

But at the same time, she announced the developers had consented to an immediate EPA investigation of their central disposal site with this caveat in her press release: "When the investigation is complete and they find no barrels and no contaminated sand at our disposal site, we demand Congresswoman LeBlanc issue a public apology to the development and to the people of the Marquette area for her unfounded and shameful allegations."

It pleased Velvet and Taylor that the investigation would take place immediately, but both were puzzled when the developers did not resist the EPA inspection request. They could have just dragged their feet a few more days until after the primary was over, but they didn't.

Why, they wondered?

The EPA conducted two days of sampling at the official debris dumping site designated on the development property. They then issued a public statement that they had "found no evidence of barrels or dangerous contamination at the dump site" and were "ending the investigation with no further action required."

The EPA announcement came as a relief to all those concerned about a major contamination spill, though it did not address the disappearance of the barrels. Nor were new samples taken at the beach site, as the EPA discounted the value of sand analysis so long after the "spill."

Newspaper headlines dubbed Velvet as a political opportunist seeking to tar her opponent and scare voters into voting for her based on fake news.

Despite Velvet's contention that the beach site had been "scrubbed" and that further analysis was needed, Lorraine flooded the airwaves with demands that Velvet withdraw from the race because of her reckless and libelous claims, hinting also that a defamation lawsuit by the developers was likely.

CHAPTER TEN

Summer Judgment and the August Primary Defeat

"After the ship has sunk, everyone knows how she might have been saved."

—Italian Proverb

MARQUETTE MICHIGAN
THE AUGUST 2024 PRIMARY

MINUTES AFTER THE POLLS CLOSED, LORRAINE WAS DECLARED THE winner of the August Democratic primary. She would face the former Republican incumbent in November, who easily defeated two minor opponents.

Final voting totals gave Lorraine 60 percent of the Democratic primary vote, a stunning trouncing of Velvet. Lorraine had not only won the overwhelming support of traditional Democratic voters but also a significant share of core Velvet voters—students and environmentalists.

The day after the primary, Velvet met with Taylor, Wenonah, and Amy to determine their path forward. Two issues they knew had been weights on the campaign: her lack of visibility in the district because of financial constraints and her failed mining permit effort.

"But I think it was the barrel issue that finally sank us," Wenonah told Velvet.

Many outside observers concurred with Wenonah. It appeared to both students and environmentalists alike that Velvet had used scare tactics and amped up student illnesses to gain a political advantage over her primary opponent.

"I agree with Wenonah," said Taylor, "but I think there is something more to the barrel issue."

He explained when he met with Lorraine, she took him on a tour of the entire Gitche Gumee real estate development. The eastern part of the development already had several dozen condominiums completed with roads and curbs. The developers officially designated the southern portion for dumping to fill in a low-lying area for future construction.

However, the western portion of the development was still in an undeveloped state, except for a newly paved parking lot at the very edge of the development boundary where they parked trucks and other machinery.

"What has that got to do with the barrel issue?" Amy asked.

"Well, I asked Lorraine why they chose the western site for paving since it was so remote, and she told me they needed a place to keep ugly, heavy equipment out of sight. I still thought the marshy site was a strange location for a paved parking lot, but until now, I didn't think any more about it."

"What are you implying?" Velvet asked.

"Well, when the EPA found no evidence of the barrels or the contaminated sand in the designated dump site, I asked myself where else they could be?" Taylor smiled with a knowing look in his eyes.

"You think it's buried under that pavement?" Velvet exclaimed.

The four all stared at each other in astonishment.

"Why didn't you bring this up before election day?" Amy demanded.

"The EPA announcement of no contamination came so close to the primary date that I felt it would look like a last gasp allegation that would only further alienate voters. And it was only a hunch, with no time to inspect the area before the election," Taylor replied. "But since then, I found additional information that makes me very suspicious of this site," he continued.

"Like what?" Velvet asked.

"I checked local paving companies for information about who had done the paving. I found the company contracted to do the paving and learned they had done it on 'an expedited basis'—within two days after the barrels were discovered."

Taylor now had the full attention of the group, as he leaned forward and continued.

"I also learned that the developers explicitly required that beach sand be deposited under the pavement and that it should not be screened or disturbed in any way. When I inquired about this provision, the paving company said it was their policy to screen out any debris from the sand, but they were told to bury the sand as it was."

"Do you think they buried the barrels and sand together under the pavement, then?" Velvet pressed.

"I asked if there were any barrels in the excavated sand and the paving company rep said no," Taylor replied.

The faces of the group dropped, but then Taylor added a proviso.

"HOWEVER, the paving company rep said that there was a Corps of Engineers transport vehicle at the beach site when they excavated the beach sand."

"So, you think the Corps—" Velvet began, but was interrupted by Taylor.

"I think the Corps has the barrels, but the contaminated soil is buried under that parking lot," Taylor responded, finishing Velvet's sentence.

"My God!" Velvet cried out. "But how can we prove this, Taylor? I lost the primary, so do I have any credibility asking for another investigation?"

The group chattered excitedly, while Velvet tried to unwrap the implications of a cover-up by the Corps.

Then Velvet stood and signaled for their attention.

"Hold on, everyone. Taylor, you seem to have this pretty well flushed out. Do you have any ideas on how I should handle this?" Velvet asked.

"Well," Taylor replied, "there are a few key questions YOU need to answer before we consider taking any action. Number one: What if the Corps had dumped many more barrels than they had reported, and what if they too were contaminated? Would anyone else pursue the Corps' involvement in the barrel issue if you don't?"

"Certainly not Lorraine or the Republican candidate if either one wins," Velvet replied.

Taylor smiled and continued.

"Number two: What if the developers did indeed bury this waste under the pavement and the contamination spreads to the surrounding land and water sources? Would anyone besides you act to prevent it from spreading?"

"No one would know until it was too late unless we pushed to contain it now," she responded.

"Exactly," Taylor smiled.

"And number three," Taylor asked, looking directly at Velvet. "Is there anyone besides you who would tackle the barrel issue, like maybe the Michigan Department of Environmental Quality, since if you raise it, it might sound like political sour grapes?"

Velvet shrugged, knowing the Governor controlled the MDEQ and was no friend of her campaign.

"You are the only one who has a reason and the will to push this investigation forward," Taylor concluded. "There will be immediate blow-back; but if you are right, you could save the land and lake we all love."

"But can I be effective as a lame duck member of Congress?" she asked the group.

"You could if you were to seek re-election as a write-in candidate in the general election. At least you would be more than a lame duck seeking answers," Wenonah responded.

"Could I win, Wenonah?" Velvet asked.

"Well, an independent, write-in campaign is a real long shot, but look at it this way: what have you got to lose? It's unlikely that either Lorraine or the Republican nominee will push an investigation before the general election, if at all."

"But if you were still a player in the election," Taylor interjected, "you would have a voice in all this, and the media would have to cover you."

"So, should I do a write-in campaign?" Velvet asked the group.

They all nodded in agreement.

Wenonah piped in, "It will be the longest of long shots, but I'm with you, sis."

"OK, what do I need to do to run as a write-in candidate?" Velvet asked.

Amy and Taylor agreed to explore the deadlines and requirements for initiating a write-in campaign at the state level, while Wenonah agreed to research third-party federal election campaign requirements.

"You must act quickly," Wenonah warned. "The November election is less than three months away."

The meeting adjourned. While awaiting the results of their research, Velvet weighed the viability of a write-in campaign. Am I just spitting into the wind, she asked herself?

However, she took solace in knowing that whatever the outcome, she was acting to protect Gitche Gumee and not just seeking a political win.

Then Gitche Gumee grabbed the spotlight again.

* * *

On a stormy Labor Day weekend, seven more 55-gallon barrels like the ones pictured in Jamal's photos washed ashore on a beach close to her home in Christmas. Unlike the barrels recovered previously, these barrels were even thicker and largely unmarked.

A beachcomber on Facebook posted a picture of the barrels, creating a stampede of curiosity seekers who were aware of the earlier barrel controversy. Local police sealed off the beach and a regional MDEQ official arrived to examine them.

Federal officials from the U.S. Corps of Engineers appeared within a few hours of the reported discovery and began removing the barrels from the beach. The barrels were undamaged and heavy, suggesting the contents were still intact.

A tug of war began as the MDEQ and the Corps both claimed custody of the barrels. The Corps claimed they owned the barrels: more munitions debris from a dumping a half century ago. But the barrels were unmarked, save again for a small line of numbers etched on the bottom.

The MDEQ claimed authority since they were found within the high-water mark of Lake Superior and were the property of the state.

However, the custody barrel ended that same day when the Republican Governor ordered the MDEQ to defer to the Corps' claim of ownership.

Battle lines then shifted to the national level, and the EPA re-entered the picture.

The EPA Great Lakes regional office wanted to inspect the barrels to determine whether they posed health or environmental risks to shoreline residents. An EPA official disclosed in a radio interview that they were negotiating with the Corps for the right to inspect the barrel contents.

Velvet called Wenonah when she learned of this national tug of war over ownership of the barrels.

By claiming ownership of the barrels, the Corps gave credence to past reports that the number and location of barrel disposal sites in Lake Superior was grossly understated. How else could heavy barrels sunk near Duluth,

Minnesota, decades ago now be washing ashore hundreds of nautical miles away in Christmas?

Second, if the EPA could gain custody of the barrels and independently analyze their contents, the decades-old question of whether the Corps dumped radioactive or toxic chemical waste into the lake decades ago finally could be answered.

However, the national barrel custody battle also ended swiftly, with the White House ordering the EPA to withdraw its demand for the barrels and recognize the Corps' sole ownership.

The Corps whisked away the barrels and later issued a press statement claiming they examined the barrel contents and that they contained nothing more than "munitions waste and other nonhazardous materials." The barrels and their contents were then "properly disposed of."

Case closed?

Not in the minds of Wenonah and Velvet. Why would the White House swoop down on this relatively minor local issue when they previously refused to address the Marquette debris weeks before? Both felt this swift action was highly suspicious.

Now, finding the lost barrels that the NMU students had recovered or the contaminated sand became imperative.

The EPA was the only federal agency that seemed concerned about the barrels. But would it be willing to further investigate the barrel issue after losing to the Corps and bowing to White House intervention?

Velvet asked Wenonah for a political read on that possibility.

"I think the EPA will become involved again only if we find a non-political basis for it to intervene. Is there a different environmental angle we could pursue?" Wenonah replied.

"Let me call Taylor. He might have an idea based on his environmental research," Velvet volunteered.

And Taylor did have an idea, although it involved the MDEQ and not the EPA.

"The remote western site that was paved over was marshy and was filled so quickly that the developers could not have had time to get a permit to fill the area," Taylor explained.

"Are you thinking it might be a wetland violation?" Velvet asked.

"Yep, the EPA delegated wetland authority to the MDEQ, and the developers would need a permit from the MDEQ before it could pave over a wetland. If someone filed a valid complaint, the MDEQ could require the site to be restored to its original state," Taylor exclaimed.

"And that would mean removing the pavement and whatever lies below it," Velvet added.

"Precisely," Taylor replied.

They had a new plan. Now they needed to determine if the paved site was a wetland. And was there someone outside their campaign who could file a complaint with the MDEQ for its unauthorized filling? That would take the politics out of the investigation.

Now Velvet had an idea.

"I'll call an NMU professor I know who is a biologist specializing in wetlands. She could help us determine whether that low-lying area is a wetland."

"Also ask the professor whether there are any maps or locational evidence of wetlands in the Gitche Gumee Estates development," Taylor suggested.

Velvet made the call. It did not take long for the professor to find wetlands in the development project, and she reported her findings to Velvet within an hour of her call.

There were several wetland-designated areas in the development, she told Velvet, and they all had been permitted or protected—except for the extreme western edge of the development, which was not scheduled to be developed.

"But that is where they put the paved parking lot, at the edge of this remote lowland," Velvet exclaimed.

"Then it's likely an illegal development," the professor responded. "But someone needs to report this wetland violation issue to trigger an MDEQ investigation."

Velvet asked Taylor to find out who owned the property next to the western edge of the development and thus could file a complaint about the illegal filling of an adjacent wetland.

Taylor checked with county officials, who gave him the names of all property owners on the western boundary of the development. There were several adjacent property owners, but one was a First American named Joel Paquin, who had been a previous supporter of Joe and his Congressional campaign.

When Taylor disclosed the names of the landowners, Velvet exclaimed at the mention of Joel Paquin.

"I know Joel, and I'm calling him right now."

Velvet had met Joel several times before and was comfortable calling him for help. Joel agreed to file a complaint both with the MDEQ and with the EPA about the paving, not just to help Velvet, but also because he was not happy about having a paved parking lot near his property line.

The wait began. Would the MDEQ investigate?

Receiving the complaint in late September, complete with pictures of the paved site, wetland maps supplied by the NMU professor, and apparent signs of wetland vegetation surrounding it, the MDEQ sent a letter to the developers on September 30 asking for more information about the paved lot.

The developers failed to respond. After a week passed, they were sent a second letter. The letter warned that because of the lack of a response from an earlier request; the MDEQ intended to send an investigative team to examine the site.

This time, the developers' attorney shot a letter back to the MDEQ, denying them access to the site without a warrant.

However, with ample evidence of a potential wetland violation, a search warrant was promptly issued in early October. Under the watchful eye of the developers, a team of MDEQ scientists began examining the soil surrounding the remote paved lot for evidence of wetland disruption.

Velvet's biology professor friend intervened at a crucial time. The professor knew a member of the MDEQ investigation team and asked if she could assist the team using her knowledge of local wetlands. As the agency was already short-handed, the team welcomed her presence, and she went to work.

She explained to the MDEQ investigative team that this low-lying area might have been an early dumping site for toxic waste from earlier mining activity, providing the team with news clippings from the 1950s showing a frequent practice of dumping such waste in nearby "swamps" like this area. Therefore, she argued, they should identify any potentially hazardous waste beneath the pavement before the team came in physical contact with the underlying soil.

Using some newly acquired and highly sophisticated detection equipment, the professor scanned the pavement surface and found evidence of suspicious contaminants below it. She proposed removal of a 20-foot square area of the pavement where the contamination appeared most concentrated to determine the nature of the contaminants below.

The developers objected again and filed another lawsuit to block the extraction. After an expedited hearing based on what the MDEQ declared was a potential emergency removal action and because of the increased local media interest in this issue, the judge ruled in favor of the excavation, only he narrowed the size of the extraction and required temporary repair of the hole pending a final decision on the wetland violation issue.

So, in late October, removal of a small section of the pavement began, as did removal of a sample of the sand below it. Chemical analysis revealed the sand was indeed from the shoreline beach where the barrels were found and that there was a significant amount of low-level radioactive waste and toxic chemicals embedded in it.

The MDEQ announced plans to excavate the entire pavement, and this time the developers did not object. The MDEQ cut into a large section of the pavement and extracted the lost contaminated beach sand, providing the missing link to the NMU student illnesses.

It didn't take long for the press to connect the claim of barrel ownership by the Corps to the contaminated sand. The early pre-election November headlines renewed allegations of a Corps cover-up of Lake Superior dumping in the 1950s and 1960s, re-opening an old environmental wound and sparking outrage by the environmental community and shoreline owners alike.

The local headlines turned their attention to the First Congressional District election, and the restored credibility of Velvet LeBlanc, along with damning complicity in the cover-up by Lorraine, the Democratic primary victor.

Connie was furious at the headlines, seeing her party's nominee again being sunk by a last-minute scandal. "The timing of this disclosure is handing the First District seat back to the Republicans," she was quoted as telling her party regulars.

Coming just days before the November general election, it was unclear what impact this scandal would have on Velvet's write-in campaign. The last polls taken in mid-October showed Velvet down 12 points to Lorraine and 11 points to her Republican challenger.

Did exposing the barrel cover-up come too late?

CHAPTER ELEVEN

The Morning After

"It ain't over until every vote is counted."

—Joe Biden

SAULT STE MARIE, MICHIGAN
POST-ELECTION DAY, NOVEMBER 2024

IT WAS THE MORNING AFTER THE NOVEMBER ELECTION.

As Velvet lay in bed in a dark room reeking of stale tobacco smoke, only small shafts of sunlight peeking through the faded curtain panels were able to penetrate its darkness. A poorly tuned radio station playing a haunting Gordon Lightfoot song further added to the alien atmosphere.

Confused and squinting, she tried to recall how she ended up in this unfamiliar room. She smelled the scent of a man's cologne on the large maroon jersey she was wearing

Then, a chill shot down her spine when she tried to roll off the bed and discovered a shirtless man lying on top of the bedcovers next to her.

Darkness concealed his face, but tiny beams of sunlight glistened off his chest and arms, including his forearm, which bore a "CHIPS" tattoo. Looking down at the jersey she was wearing, which had CMU initials emblazoned on it, Velvet now recognized her bedmate.

"Taylor! What are you doing in my bed?" she shouted.

The prone occupant sprang up with bleary eyes, awakened from a sound sleep.

"Velvet, are you all right?" he asked.

He reached over to turn on the bedside lamp, sitting up and smiling at her.

"I'm glad you rejoined the living," he chuckled.

"Taylor," Velvet stammered in confusion, "I repeat, what are you doing in my bed?"

"This is my bed, Velvet."

"What?" Velvet blurted out in surprise.

"You don't remember last night?" Taylor responded. "When the networks called your race just after the polls closed, you grabbed my hand and told me you needed to get out of the casino victory party room. I asked where and you said you didn't care, as long as it was some place no one could find you."

"I don't remember that," she replied in astonishment.

"Well, anyway, I took you here to my hotel room to give you some privacy."

"When we got to my room, you said you needed a drink, which surprised me since I have rarely seen you drink anything alcoholic. I only had a bottle of cheap whiskey, but you downed two shots and got violently ill."

"But," Velvet continued, "my clothes—why am I wearing your CMU jersey and how did I end up in your bed?"

"I had to take off your clothes, as they were covered with vomit. I carried you into the bathroom to clean you up."

"You mean you undressed me?" Velvet exclaimed.

"Only to get you out of your vomit-soaked clothes, Velvet. I couldn't let you sleep in them."

"I still don't remember any of this," Velvet interrupted.

Rising from the bed, she stumbled to the window. Partially opening one of the drapery panels, she peered at a snow-covered parking lot, dusted by an Alberta clipper that had passed through overnight.

Tears trickled down her cheeks as the reality of her political plight hit home. I will soon be a former member of Congress.

Gitche Gumee, I have failed you, she moaned to herself.

Taylor walked over and put his hands gently on her shoulders.

With his touch, time stood still for a merciful moment. It was as though Joe had returned to this youthful body and reminded her of how much she missed the physical comfort of her late husband.

She turned and embraced Taylor, reliving thoughts of her last intimate evening with Joe before she left Washington. Her arms wrapped around his waist and she rested her head on his chest, feeling his heart beating as rapidly as hers in this tender moment.

But just at that moment, a sharp knock on the door brought them both back to reality. The compromising position in which they found themselves, her embracing Taylor in front of their hotel window, caused them both to scurry for their clothes.

Velvet fled to the bathroom, donning a bathrobe and pulling off his jersey.

"Taylor, is Velvet in there?" the voice continued. "Please open the door. I have to find her," Wenonah pleaded from the hallway.

"I'll be right there, Wenonah," Taylor responded, taking his time to get to the door to give Velvet time to adjust her robe and him time to retrieve his jersey.

"Hurry, this is incredible," Wenonah stammered, continuing to pound on the door.

Taylor opened the door, his jersey in hand.

"Do you know where Velvet …" her voice tailed off as Velvet emerged from the bathroom in a bathrobe.

"What's so important, and how did you track me down here?" Velvet cried defensively, half in frustration and half in embarrassment at her compromising situation.

"I'm sorry, but the hotel valet told me you were last seen leaving the campaign party with Taylor," Wenonah blurted out in frustration. "We looked everywhere else before figuring you had to be here."

Then, watching as a shirtless Taylor disappeared into the bathroom, she gasped, "I didn't know that you—"

"There is nothing to know, Wenonah. Now what's so important?"

"Read this." Wenonah thrust her iPhone into her sister's face.

Velvet stared in disbelief at the news headline on the screen: "LeBlanc pulls upset: Late vote tally gives her narrow win."

Her long shot, write-in Congressional campaign, which pollsters and pundits alike declared DOA, had emerged phoenix-like as one of the major congressional upsets of 2024.

"I won?" Velvet screamed.

"Yes, you did, sis!" Wenonah shouted back.

"Staff members, supporters, and members of the press all have been waiting downstairs for a statement. Your Republican and Democrat opponents have already called to concede. I've been on the phone all morning with state party officials and it's true—you won!" Wenonah repeated.

Velvet was still in a state of disbelief. *Did I really win, or is this another cruel joke?*

"I laid some clothes on the bed in your room down the hall. You need to change before anyone sees you here. Let's go!" Wenonah shouted in triumph.

Seeing the excitement in Wenonah's eyes, Velvet's sadness dissipated. She had not been this excited since her April special election victory.

Velvet hugged her sister and dashed out of Taylor's room, running down the hall to her room in her bathrobe.

Wenonah then strode into Taylor's bathroom, staring at him in disbelief.

"Did you screw my sister?" she demanded.

Taylor glared at her. But before he could respond, Wenonah continued her angry confrontation.

"Never mind. Take off that wrinkled jersey and put on some decent clothes."

As Taylor peeled off the jersey and headed to his closet, Wenonah followed and continued to chastise him.

"And don't let anyone see you alone with her again. What were you thinking by taking her to your hotel room? We've been given a second political chance, so let's not blow it with a sleazy tabloid story."

Wenonah then peered out the still open hotel room door, monitoring who was walking down the hall or who might have been within earshot of her conversation with Taylor and Velvet. She saw a maid cart next to an open door two rooms down the hall and heard a door slam, but nothing else.

After texting Amy that she had found Velvet, she stood in the hallway and waited for Taylor to change his clothes.

Meanwhile, Velvet looked with disdain at the woman's business suit Wenonah had placed on her bed. Another bow to the political establishment, she thought.

She badly needed to bathe, so she threw off her bathrobe and dashed into the shower, covering her hair and green headband with a plastic shower cap, as there was no time to wash and dry it.

After a brief shower, she grabbed a towel and dashed out of the bathroom, hastily throwing on her clothes. As she was combing her hair, tying it into a ponytail and adjusting her headband, she glanced at the muted television screen in her room to see if there was any news of her upset win.

The local election results were overshadowed by a more politically significant and newsworthy national event which had been unfolding overnight, summarized by a rolling "Breaking News" banner at the bottom of the screen: "Presidential election still undecided: no victor declared."

"Wenonah," Velvet shouted down the hall. "What's this about the Presidential election being too close to call?"

Wenonah trotted down the hall to calm Velvet, with Taylor close behind.

"We'll fill you in soon, Velvet. But first, get ready to take a bow as the newly re-elected congresswoman from the First District before other national events overshadow your victory."

"Wenonah! The press can wait! I have so many questions."

"All right, I'll text Tom to come up and give you the facts as he knows them."

With that, Velvet sat on the edge of her bed, gazing at the television screen in anticipation.

I feel like Rip Van Winkle who just awoke.

When Tom received Wenonah's text, he broke off his conversation with a staffer and rushed to Velvet's hotel room. Filled with excitement, he already had plans for a new legislative agenda.

As he entered the room, Wenonah, Amy, and Taylor were already there, high fiving each other. Velvet hugged him in excitement.

"Tom, did I really win this? Every poll said I wouldn't, and the race was called so early last night,"

"I just confirmed the final numbers," Tom smiled. He then gave her a thumbs up.

"OMG!" Velvet shouted.

Before Tom could elaborate, Velvet's acting press secretary, Angela, stormed in and marched directly towards Velvet.

"Velvet, you've got to come downstairs to the press conference room now before everyone leaves. State and local television and radio reporters are packing up since there's been no sign of you. I've been trying to keep them there, but I'm afraid they're done waiting," Angela fretted.

"Wait a minute," Velvet exclaimed. "Why isn't my race important enough to keep local reporters waiting a bit longer?"

"Everyone calm down." Amy shouted. "Look, we need to seize this moment and use it to our advantage. No sense in stumbling through the press conference without giving Velvet some ammo."

Velvet nodded her approval.

"Now, as I see it," Amy began, "there are several questions that are sure to come up in the press conference, so let's make sure we address these first before CONGRESSWOMAN LEBLANC talks to the press. One: Did your own internal polls tell you something that the national polls didn't and why did you leave the victory party room early last night? Two: Was your barrel investigation a planned October surprise, and do you think it was why you won? Three: With whom will you caucus when you take office as an independent: the Democrats or the Republicans? Four: What do you think about the Presidential race?"

"Good questions. Amy. Angela, can you buy me fifteen minutes? I need to be brought up to speed on all of this," Velvet asked.

"I'll try, but what shall I tell them is the reason for the delay?" Angela replied in exasperation.

"Tell them I have some personal calls to make, and they are taking longer than expected," Velvet replied.

Angela bolted out of the hotel room and downstairs to the improvised press conference room, while Velvet resumed her impromptu pre-press conference briefing.

"Tell me about the polling surprise questions first," Velvet directed.

Tom explained that the inaccurate polling resulted from a string of unique and unexpected events that dramatically altered voting in the last few days of the campaign.

"I can discuss this in more detail, but point to Taylor's student organizational efforts, which were overlooked and underestimated by the media."

"OK, but what if they ask about my absence over the last twelve hours? How can I tell them I thought I was going to win if I didn't stay in the room?" Velvet asked sheepishly.

"Turn that question around by pointing out that all the media polling had predicted your defeat. Talk about your student voter registration efforts, which you had been counting on but which weren't tallied until long after the polls were closed. You were just waiting for those key votes to be tallied," Tom counseled.

"Cleverly put," Velvet smiled. "I will dodge the October surprise question by saying the timing of the investigation was NOT political, but I will agree that it affected the election. However, I won't know how significant an impact it had until after we examine the final vote count."

"Also tell them that the real October surprise was the late ruling by the state supreme court allowing same-day voter registration in Michigan," Tom added. "The ruling caused a wave of unregistered student voters to appear at the voting sites on election day. The decision wreaked havoc among local election officials in counties with large universities."

"Good," Velvet nodded. "So, students came to my aid, and the pollsters didn't see it coming."

"Then there was a problem with the state ballot counting process."

Velvet cut him off. "Tom, you are going too far into the political weeds. I get the picture of a last-minute rush of student voting and the delays in the vote-counting process that set in motion my eventual win. But give me some hard polling numbers."

"Well, the early voting reported at 8:15 pm last night put your Republican opponent at 38 percent, Lorraine at twenty-eight percent, and you at twenty-one percent. The other two minor party candidates shared the rest of the votes.

"Strangely, I now remember those ugly numbers," Velvet interrupted.

"Well, those percentages reflected only forty percent of the votes counted, and I talked with a press friend of mine who disclosed that the media assumed the late counted votes from the university counties would be equally divided between you and Lorraine. They assumed on that basis that a seventeen percent deficit was too great to overcome and called the race for the Republican."

"And they got it wrong!" Velvet interjected with satisfaction.

Tom nodded.

"Now, as to the other numbers you need to know, updated poll numbers later in the evening put the race as a statistical dead heat, with you and your Republican opponent each polling at thirty-nine percent. Lorraine's vote total had dwindled to fifteen percent."

"When I heard the news, we all bolted back to the 'Victory Party' room," Amy added. "We saw only forty-six votes separated you from your Republican opponent."

Amy paused and Velvet smiled at her sister, who had just winked at her.

"With eight percent of the vote still not tallied, I called a friend on TV 9-10 and asked whether the vote totals were still incomplete. After what seemed to be an eternity, my friend called me back and said there were still a substantial number of outstanding votes from university counties," Amy continued.

"That's when we looked for Taylor," Wenonah added, "as we recognized victory rested with the university student turnout, and Taylor was in the best position to tell us what to expect from his organizational efforts."

"I called Taylor's cell phone and yours," Wenonah explained, "but got no response from either call."

"When the local television stations ended local coverage at 2 am, you were still trailing, but only by a handful of votes. And there were still three percent of the votes left to count—all from the university counties," Amy added.

"With no new numbers likely to be reported for several hours and since I couldn't find either you or Taylor, I went to my hotel room to catch a few hours of sleep before renewing my efforts to get final vote totals and then find you. But I couldn't be certain whether the final numbers would reverse your earlier media projected loss," Tom explained.

Wenonah jumped in. "When we couldn't find you, I checked with Frank and then began calling neighbors in Christmas to check and see if you had gone there. I also discreetly began asking those at the victory party whether they had seen you. Like Amy, I was tired, so I fell asleep in a lounge chair waiting for a call from anyone to help me find you.

"At 6 am, the final votes were tabulated and the news on the internet sent whoops of joy from the few staffers still in the casino hallway, waking me up," Wenonah added. "The votes of the remaining newly registered student voters were finally counted and gave you a forty-one percent to thirty-nine percent win over the Republican, with Lorraine and two write-in candidates trailing far behind."

"Then we began an all-out search for our re-elected congresswoman," Amy added. "So, it wasn't as though we didn't try to find you earlier to tell you all this."

"Until we found you in TAYLOR'S room!" Wenonah barked.

Both Amy and Wenonah then looked first at Velvet and then at Taylor. Other campaign staff members who had wandered into Velvet's room while the briefing was taking place squirmed as they read the body language of both Taylor and Velvet.

Then, after an awkward pause, Velvet grimaced and changed the subject.

"I am going to dodge whether I will caucus with the Democrats or Republicans until after I talk to both party leaders."

"Good, and let's talk about the Presidential election later, as time is of the essence to get to the press conference," Amy interrupted. "It's a razor thin close race. Just tell them you'll be watching to see whether recounts in a few states will decide it."

"Now, are there any other key questions we've overlooked?"

"No, I think that's all I need right now," Velvet replied.

"All right, then let's hurry down to the press conference."

Velvet nodded in agreement.

"Tell everyone to head down to the press conference and I'll join them shortly. I need to catch my breath," Velvet replied.

Velvet stepped into her bathroom, looking at the mirror. Seeing the rather dour look on her face, she wondered why she was not happier at this moment of victory?

Her heart ached for guidance from her spiritual family. So many questions went through her mind.

What would my parents, who were so poorly treated when they ran for office, think of my victory?

What would Joe have said about my campaign?

What would Abequa have thought about my new journey?

She longed for answers, but she knew they would have to wait until after the press conference.

Exiting her room, she took the elevator down to the main floor and marched to the podium in the converted press conference room. By now, the room was only sparsely populated by the press, so she made a few comments about the historic nature of her win and thanked her supporters. She then opened the briefing for questions.

After taking a few softball questions, a local reporter asked her what she thought her parents would have said about her election.

Velvet paused and smiled at the reporter. "Great question. That's exactly what I plan to find out. I am going to reconnect with my spiritual family right now. Thank you all for coming and I will issue a formal statement later today."

She then stepped away from the podium and marched out of the room, much to the surprise of everyone, including her staff.

There were shouts by reporters as she left, but she did not respond. Her staff members stood in stunned silence as she exited.

It was time, she decided, to return to her spiritual home at the old Mission Hill Cemetery.

CHAPTER TWELVE

Seeking the Spiritual Bond

"They are not dead who live in the hearts they leave behind."

—Tuscarora

SAULT STE. MARIE, MICHIGAN
POST-ELECTION DAY PRESS CONFERENCE AFTERMATH

"WHERE DID VELVET GO?" AMY AND ANGELA BOTH EXCLAIMED IN unison, looking frantically up and down the casino hallways after Velvet abruptly left the press conference.

"Damn it," Amy shouted. "We've got to find her. We need more news coverage before the Presidential election swallows up the entire news cycle."

Amy and Angela scoured the main floor lobby and hallways for Velvet, opening doors to conference rooms and nosing into restaurants and bars. Not finding her on the main floor, they rushed back upstairs to her hotel room.

But Velvet had bolted out a side door into the casino parking lot, walking down the parking rows in search of her distinctively green campaign car.

When she glanced back and saw Angela and Wenonah rush out the front door of the casino, she ducked for cover. They'll not stop me from my spiritual family reunion, she decided. Spotting the green campaign car near the rear entrance to the parking lot, she rushed towards it. Then she knelt beside it and texted Taylor.

"Meet me at the campaign car in the parking lot now—urgent! Don't tell anyone!"

Taylor had joined the staff posse looking for Velvet when he received her text. He had to choose between telling Amy or obeying Velvet's command for secrecy with only a split-second to decide. He excused himself from the hunt on the pretext of needing to get a warmer coat from the campaign car.

He jogged through the parking lot and, as he approached the campaign car, he saw Velvet crouched down on the passenger side.

"Taylor, please don't talk. Just get in the car," Velvet whispered.

"Where are we going?" Taylor asked.

"To old Mission Hill Cemetery. I need some time with my family."

Taylor climbed into the car, and Velvet crawled into the back seat. They then slipped out of the parking lot.

"Velvet, you know the staff is combing the casino trying to find you. Can I at least tell Amy you're OK?" Taylor pleaded.

"I'll text Amy and Wenonah and let them know you and I will be back to the casino in a couple of hours," Velvet promised.

"But they're already angry at me for taking you to my room last night. What will they think—"

"Please just drive, Taylor. I'll straighten things out with them in due time, but first I need some family bonding."

Taylor sighed in resignation and began their journey.

Velvet closed her eyes and settled in for the ride to the cemetery.

When Amy received Velvet's text, she was furious. She was still angry at Velvet for cutting out of the press conference early.

Wenonah was angry too, but with Taylor for being alone with Velvet again despite her warning.

Amy returned to the press conference room to survey the damage done. Since it was empty, she had Angela email her press contacts to tell them that Velvet would issue a follow-up statement soon. She then texted her staff and told them there would be a staff meeting that afternoon.

With her boss AWOL, Amy sat down in a conference room chair and waited impatiently to hear from Velvet. A few minutes later, Wenonah plunked down beside her.

"I think I know where Velvet is," Wenonah confided.

"Well, where the hell is she?" Amy shouted.

"I bet she's gone to old Mission Hill Cemetery to be with our parents. She seeks refuge there in times of great stress. Her spiritual needs are far greater than the politics of the moment."

"But she has lost such an important media moment," Amy whined.

"Well, this may work to her advantage, as it has created a sense of mystery about her sudden departure. When the press finds out she went to be with her deceased parents, it also may create a wave of public sympathy. Might be a good storyline about her candidacy," Wenonah added.

Amy paused and then smiled at the prospect.

"All right," Amy agreed, "but we're going to have a serious 'Come to Jesus' moment when she gets back."

* * *

As Taylor slowed down to navigate up the steep incline leading to the cemetery, Velvet awoke feeling hopeful. I soon will be with my family in my time of triumph. After Taylor parked the car in the look-out parking area across from the cemetery, Velvet threw open the door and sprang from the back seat.

"Wait here, Taylor," Velvet shouted as she ran towards the cemetery monuments.

Her first stop was a memorial stone with the names of her parents, Arnold and Margaret LeBlanc. The inscribed message below their names read:

"Now resting in the arms of Gitche Gumee"

November 6, 2007."

Velvet knelt before the memorial plaque and pressed her head and hands against it, her dangling black hair contrasting with the white blanket of snow covering the top of the monument.

She thought back to happy times when her parents were the voices of the U.P. environmental movement. She remembered the joy of following their political exhortations with songs and the simple but happy life she had enjoyed.

Closing her eyes, she prayed aloud to the spirits of her parents.

"My beloved family, please guide me so that I can carry on your mission," Velvet said in a soft voice.

And for just one glorious moment, it was as though they were a family again, embraced by the warmth of their spirits amidst the cold cemetery winter scene.

A squirrel brushed past her while she was kneeling, interrupting Velvet's momentary family reunion. But her spiritual needs had been fulfilled, as she had bridged the gap between her earthly reality and the spiritual embrace of her deceased parents.

Arising from her parents' memorial, she then moved to the next row where her aunt was buried, now marked by a spirit house Frank had made for her.

Kneeling, she spoke softly, "Oh Auntie, I know my life is not what you wanted for me, but I know this is a far better thing I'm doing now than I've ever done before. You've given me the strength and knowledge I needed to make this new journey, and I love you for all you've done for me."

Velvet removed a locket from her neck containing a picture of her parents and left it on the shelf of her aunt's spirit house.

There was one more spiritual contact she wanted to visit in a newer section of the cemetery.

Turning from Abequa's grave, she walked across a path and toward a large stone monument emblazoned with the word "Johnson."

She approached the monument but did not kneel, as a torrent of memories overcame her. He represented the more recent political phase of her life, and the pain that came with their journey together.

It was Joe who wanted to take on the establishment, and she was to be his willing partner. Revelations of his infidelity sabotaged their political journey, leaving her to blaze her path alone.

She stood motionless, reflecting upon the alien political world she had entered and now inherited.

Just then, a hand touched her shoulder.

"Let's go sit in the car and get warm," Taylor encouraged.

Velvet turned and nodded. She now felt the winter cold after her warm family interlude. The two walked together to the car, where they sat for several minutes without talking, gazing at the distant northern Canadian landscape below.

As she sat staring at the back of Taylor's head, Velvet's thoughts drifted to the personal role he had played in her campaign. He had worked with Joe when Joe was a tribal council member. When Mount Pleasant was added to the First District's political boundaries, Joe hired him as a Congressional staff member, a decision that saved Joe's life in his first months in office.

She had grown to rely on Taylor more and more after Joe's passing. I am so grateful he is with me now, she thought.

Now spiritually refreshed, she returned to the reality of her current situation.

The Great Spirit has given me a second chance to do what Joe and I set out to do in 2022. I must try again, she thought.

"Let's get back to the casino, Taylor," she said. "I have work to do."

It was a long, silent trip back. But Velvet brought back with her the spiritual inspiration she needed.

* * *

When Velvet and Taylor arrived at the casino front entrance, the stern faces of Amy and Wenonah greeted them.

"Velvet, do you know—" Amy began.

But before Amy could complete her sentence, Velvet put her finger to her lips as she passed by and walked into the casino lobby. She beckoned for Amy and Wenonah to follow her to a secluded corner of a nearby empty conference room, where she squatted on the floor.

Wenonah pulled Taylor aside on their way into the casino, warning him, "Don't you ever cross me again! I told you never to be alone with her. There's too much at stake."

Taylor expected the fury, but knew this was not the time to argue, so he took the tongue lashing without responding and followed Velvet and Amy into the casino.

As they squatted together on the floor, Amy regained her composure and expressed her frustrations in more measured tones. Then she handed Velvet a long list of callers eager to talk with her after her election.

"All right, you have a lot of calls to make," Amy asserted.

Velvet nodded, acknowledging the political ritual of being a gracious victorious candidate, and headed to her hotel room with Amy to make the calls. But after reviewing the long list of callers and their suggested priority, she recoiled at the task.

"Amy, while I understand the need to reply to the concession calls from my Republican opponent and Lorraine, I have no desire now to return calls from the Governor or other elected officials who were of little help to me, nor to the press which abandoned me in the later stages of the campaign."

Instead, she skipped down the list and began making personal calls to tribal members and student organizational leaders whom she believed were the keys to her victory. She reveled in their warm support, and it was apparent after two lengthy conversations that the calling list would take a considerable amount of time to complete.

"Amy, I don't have time today to do the follow-up calls with most of the press contacts you listed. Please say I will get back to them as soon as I can."

Amy was aghast. First Velvet had skipped out of the campaign victory party on election night, then she slipped off to the cemetery after bolting out of the abbreviated press conference that morning, and now she was blowing off any opportunity to make amends with the press with some one-on-one press calls.

"Velvet, you need the press coverage to—"

"For what? What have they done for me since Joe died?" Velvet asked.

Amy was about to reply, but Velvet continued.

"Nothing. That's what they've done. Well, they can just cool their heels while I talk to those who helped me. Sorry, Amy, but I will call them after I finish talking to my loyal friends."

Velvet was determined, so Amy texted the bad news to all her media contacts, claiming that Velvet still had some pressing personal issues she needed to address. She promised Velvet would call them as soon as possible.

Two local Soo reporters who had stayed in the casino lobby after the abbreviated press conference read Amy's text. They were not happy that they had wasted most of an early news cycle waiting for her return.

Personal issues again? What kind of personal issues could be so important, they thought.

They looked for staff members who might know Velvet's situation. They also sought contacts outside the campaign that might have some key information.

A scandal would be their new mission, and they were determined to file a story based on any granular knowledge they hoped to glean from casino employees and the insiders in Velvet's campaign. Some news was better than no news at all.

From the casino employees, the reporters learned of a shouting incident in the early morning hours on the fifth floor of the casino hotel booked by the LeBlanc for Congress campaign. They also learned that a partially clad couple had been seen embracing in a window on the same fifth floor in the early morning hours.

The reporters began quizzing other hotel staff, campaign volunteers, and almost anyone they encountered in the casino that morning to learn more about these two early morning hotel incidents. Were these incidents in any way related to Velvet's reluctance to engage with them, they wondered?

To their surprise, as they wandered through the casino, they found former field director Jim Zenger sitting alone at the bar near the casino hotel auditorium, uncharacteristically disheveled and obviously intoxicated.

They knew Jim had been a close aide to Joe and a rising star in Democratic circles for his extraordinary recruitment and field organizational skills. Whatever the reason for his departure from Velvet's campaign, it had been a stunning political setback for Jim. Jim's public backing of losing candidate Lorraine after leaving Velvet's campaign further tarnished his political resume.

So, the reporters were both wary and curious as they approached Jim at the bar.

It surprised them that Jim not only did not object to their arrival, but instead beckoned them both to sit down and join him.

After exchanging pleasantries, they asked Jim for his assessment of the November election. It surprised them when he took credit not only for Velvet's special election win in April to fill Joe's term, but also for recruiting Lorraine Sampson to defeat Velvet in the August Democratic primary.

They pressed him for more details. Why would he switch sides after the special election?

They had found Jim at a propitious time. He was reeling from Velvet's successful grassroots campaign in the general election. That was the type of organizational effort that was his key strength. He also had just learned that the state party had terminated his consulting services contract.

In his current state of extreme inebriation, he offered scandalous details about the extramarital sexual activities of former Congressman Joe Johnson and Velvet, but only on the condition of anonymity.

Just what the reporters wanted to hear.

Jim revealed that when he had served as Joe's field director, Joe would ask him to bring young women to his hotel room when he was traveling in the district without Velvet.

"Are you saying that former Congressman Joe Johnson had sex with young women on multiple occasions while you were with him?" one reporter queried.

"Look, I am not proud of what happened. I am just telling you what I know," Jim replied.

"So why did you take part in this 'sexcapade' if you knew it was wrong?"

"I kept this secret, as it gave me real job security. Joe was prone to fire people with whom he was unhappy, regardless of their skill. I felt knowledge of his infidelity was my ace in the hole."

He paused, frowning at the reporters, and then continued, intent on revenge against all whom he felt had wronged him.

"That job security ended when Joe's plane went down and staff loyal to Velvet took over," Jim added wryly. "And then there was Connie."

"Do you mean the Connie, the state party chair?" one reporter asked, seeking clarity.

"Yes, Joe had a long-standing romantic relationship with Connie. If he had not tried to return home on Christmas Eve, he would have been sleeping with Connie that evening."

The reporters looked at each other in astonishment.

"You said Representative LeBlanc had extramarital affairs. What evidence do you have of those affairs?" the second reporter asked.

"Everyone on her staff knows Taylor Grant has been sleeping with Velvet even when Joe was alive"

"Can you tell us one concrete incident to corroborate your story?" the reporters pressed.

"Well, did you see Velvet last night shortly after the election was called?" Jim asked.

The reporters shook their heads.

"And did you see Taylor during that same period last night?" he continued.

The reporters paused again, looking surprised.

"They both disappeared from the casino auditorium early on election night, didn't they?" Jim responded.

The reporters looked stunned.

"Figure it out," Jim laughed.

The disclosures floored the reporters, and they rushed to their offices to assemble a story about this sex-riddled campaign.

* * *

Within an hour after meeting with Jim, the reporters composed a draft newspaper headline for their story. Then they called Amy and summarized their story, including an allegation that Velvet was sleeping with Taylor the night of her election. They entitled their story:

"Shameless: LeBlanc Campaign Riddled with Charges of Adultery and Fornication."

Amy was floored and asked them not to publish the story before she talked with Velvet. The reporters agreed to hold the story from the print media, but that it would go on their website soon if Amy did not arrange a personal interview for them with Velvet before their reporting deadline.

Amy promised to try but threatened a lawsuit if this story were untrue. The reporters countered they had a high-level inside source and were very comfortable with the veracity of their story.

Amy then called Wenonah, describing her conversation with the reporters.

"Who do you think that high-level source is?" Amy asked Wenonah.

"I think it's Taylor," Wenonah responded. "Who else would have known what happened on election night?"

"Tell the reporters we'll call them back within the hour," Wenonah directed Amy. "I'll find Taylor."

Then began the hunt for Taylor. Both women were furious. They needed him to retract what they believed was his leak to the press before publication of the destructive story.

But he was nowhere to be found, and the deadline passed.

The story hit the paper's web page and quickly spread like wildfire on social media. Then the print version came out.

"I know it's a small consolation," Amy told Velvet after she saw the newspaper headline, "but at least it's a page three story because of the flurry of stories about the Presidential election."

But the story had deeply hurt Velvet.

It not only sullied the reputations of both Joe and her, but it also staggered her confidence in whom she could trust on her staff in the days and weeks ahead.

Who among her most trusted aides was tarnishing her election victory? And who on her staff could she still trust to help her through the difficult political transition ahead?

She knew her alleged sexual relationship with Taylor was untrue, but what of Joe's sexual relationship with the chair of the Michigan Democratic Party? Could this charge also be true, and was there still more she did not know about Joe's infidelity?

Velvet struggled between her impulse either to correct errors in the story or to ignore these staggering allegations altogether.

She called Wenonah for guidance.

"I know some parts of the story about my relationship with Taylor are false," Velvet began her phone conversation.

Wenonah warned her that attacking only parts of the story was tantamount to admitting that the rest of the story was true.

"Well, Taylor already told me about Joe's unfaithfulness on district trips, so that part of the story is probably true," Velvet protested.

"Taylor?" Wenonah exclaimed. "You're accepting his word that all this happened? I think he's the inside source of the story!"

"I can't believe it was Taylor," Velvet responded.

"Who then?" Wenonah asked. "Amy is the only other person I can think of who would have such inside information."

Velvet realized that Amy was indeed one of the few people on her current staff who could have talked to the media in great detail about these events. Was Amy complicit in this horrible secret?

Taylor had wanted Amy off the campaign. Is that the real reason Taylor lobbied to oust Amy from the campaign, she wondered?

"I can't believe Amy would be disloyal to me after all she has done for the campaign," Velvet replied.

"Well, until you figure out who the source of this story is, better to say nothing rather than try to pick apart a story that might blow up in your face," Wenonah advised.

After finishing her telephone conversation with Wenonah, a loneliness crept in that she had not experienced since Joe's death.

Velvet needed a new shoulder to lean on, so she called Frank who, as chairperson of the Sault Tribe, had no political axe to grind. Maybe he could offer comfort and sage advice at this crucial time in her political life.

But her call to him went to voice mail.

Alone in the artificial atmosphere of the Soo casino, she recalled the scandal that had engulfed the campaign of the Democratic candidate Joe and she had supported in 2020. The candidate resigned from the campaign after the disclosure of his sexual relationship with a staffer. Even though she knew at least one of the allegations against her was untrue, would resignation be the best course of action as well?

After some serious reflection, she concluded she would not resign, but neither would she remain silent. I will not let this scandalous story end my political journey. Surely the Great Spirit would not want me to quit now.

She called her sister again, but this time her line was busy, so she left her a voice mail message.

"Wenonah, I just wanted to let you know I will not respond to the story for the time being, as you advised, even though I know at least some of it is untrue. But I will be speaking out as soon as I get all the facts. I will not let this political blood sport stop me from carrying on our parents' environmental mission, regardless of the source of the story."

She knew the scandal would weaken her bargaining position with both major political parties, though she did not have a strong bargaining position to begin with since neither party needed her for control of Congress. The Republicans would still control both the House and the Senate, regardless of which party she aligned with.

In fact, would either party even offer her a desirable committee position to join their party in the new Congress, or would she be treated as damaged goods and left in the same political wilderness she had found herself prior to the November election?

As Velvet weighed how to manage her sinking political position in Washington, new political events developed in the Presidential election.

Mercifully, her scandal news faded, as the national media's primary focus was turned to the Second Congressional District in Maine, not the First District of Michigan.

Velvet would soon learn why.

CHAPTER THIRTEEN

The Maine Question

"As Maine goes, so goes the nation."

—Old political maxim

AUGUSTA, MAINE
POST NOVEMBER ELECTION DAY

VELVET WAS PUZZLED WHY THE MEDIA WAS MORE INTERESTED IN A rural Congressional race in Maine than in her stunning upset win. So, she called her sister.

"Wenonah, what's going on in Maine? Why is that congressional race so important?"

"Because it may very well decide who the next President will be," Wenonah replied.

"What?"

Wenonah explained the huge political problem facing national political leaders: how to resolve a 2024 Presidential election projected to result in an inconclusive electoral vote of 269–268–1. Without reaching the minimum 270 electoral votes, the Constitution provided the House with a little used and murky process for deciding who would become President.

"The simple solution to avoid that process would be to get that one uncommitted elector to cast his vote for the Republican nominee," Wenonah stressed.

"Let me guess, that one uncommitted elector is from Maine, right?" Velvet responded.

"Yep," Wenonah replied. "But you know, Velvet, there are some curious parallels between the Maine Congressional election and yours," Wenonah continued.

"Like what?"

"First, the Maine Second Congressional District was geographically the largest district east of the Mississippi until the 2020 redistricting made yours number one. And like your district, it is a sprawling, rural area with a troubled history of tribal casinos. And it even elected a write-in Congressman."

"Wow, that is odd," Velvet remarked.

"And Maine's new write-in Congressman is the son of the lumberjack presidential candidate, the man who holds the deciding vote in the electoral college."

"The lumberjack candidate?" Velvet laughed.

"They call him that because he lives in a town known for its huge Paul Bunyan statue. He is 80 years old and a perennial but unsuccessful candidate for many state offices. After so many election attempts, he developed a small but dedicated following. His only successful election was serving as a one-term mayor of Bangor."

"Really?" Velvet exclaimed. "I can see why I never heard of him."

"And," Wenonah added, "when he ran for President this year, he never even campaigned outside Maine."

"Why did he bother to run for President in 2024 if he had no chance of winning?"

"Well, sometimes people do things because it is the right thing to do despite overwhelming odds, like you did running a write-in campaign. He scorned the other two major presidential candidates and ran an anti-establishment campaign with the slogan 'It takes a lumberjack to clear the Washington swamp,'" Wenonah explained. "But he had no funding and no message other than he was not like the other two."

"Sounds more like ego than principle," Velvet responded. "What was this, his last hurrah?"

"Some of that, but I think there also was a strong family reason," Wenonah added. "His son shared the same first and last name, so I think his father hoped his candidacy might win his son some free publicity and sympathy votes as well. An establishment-supported state senator had defeated his son in the Democratic primary, but his son won as a write-in candidate in the general election."

"Like me!" Velvet exclaimed.

"Yep. But his son won his seat by a more comfortable margin than you."

"But what does his son's win have to do with the one electoral college vote holding up the Presidential election?" Velvet asked impatiently.

"Maine is one of only two states that doesn't award all of its electoral votes to the candidate who wins the statewide popular vote. For example, in Michigan, the candidate who wins the popular vote statewide gets all fifteen electoral votes. Maine awards its four electoral votes using a Congressional District model. Each candidate who wins one of its two Congressional Districts gets an electoral vote and whomever wins the popular vote statewide gets the other 2 electoral votes."

"So, the lumberjack's son won the Second Congressional seat, but his son is not an elector, right?" Velvet pressed.

"No, his father is the elector for the Second District."

"What? How?" Velvet shouted.

"Well, the lumberjack candidate picked up just enough votes to win the Second District Presidential popular vote and, hence, its one electoral vote. And he had already slated himself as his own elector for that district."

"Can he do that?" Velvet asked.

"The law is vague in this area, but experts say yes, he can. No one thought this was even possible, much less probable, before now," Wenonah responded.

"So, the lumberjack is an elector who could decide who the next President will be?" Velvet asked.

"Potentially yes. That's why a recount in the Second District is so important. If the recount results in the Republican Presidential candidate being declared the winner, it would give her the one additional electoral college vote needed to become President."

"That's crazy," Velvet stammered.

"Yes, but it's why all eyes are on Maine and not your election," Wenonah concluded.

"But weren't there other elections close like mine and the one in Maine? Why aren't the parties challenging elections in other states as well?"

"They are, but since the 2016 and 2020 elections, when there were wild allegations of election fraud and Russian interference, most states took steps to ensure the security and accuracy of their vote counting process," Wenonah responded. "Except Maine."

"Why not Maine?"

"Maine refused to modernize its voting system, leaving many rural voting precincts vulnerable to both human error and hacking. So, it's more likely there than anywhere else in the country that voting errors could reverse an election and decide the Presidential race."

"When will we know the outcome of the recount?"

"The Maine Secretary of State took the unusual step of starting a recount early this morning when it was apparent that the voting in the Second District was both close and very consequential, so we may know today."

"And if the recount does not change the results in the Second District?" Velvet continued. "What's next?"

"Well, the electors do not vote until mid-December. So, until then we have not actually elected our next President. The elector balloting outcome will be announced on January 6, when all the state elector ballots are officially counted by Congress with the Vice President presiding."

"But that's been routine in the past, right?" Velvet asked.

"Yes, but if no one still has 270 electoral votes on January 6, the House will elect the next President," Wenonah continued.

"Has that ever happened before?"

"Not since 1824, exactly 100 years ago," Wenonah replied,

"So, I guess we just have to wait on Maine like everyone else?" Velvet responded.

"That's about all we can do," Wenonah agreed.

"That being the case, let's sit down with staff and talk about my next steps as a member of Congress and not fixate on what I can't control," Velvet concluded.

Wenonah nodded in agreement.

"I'll ask a staff member to watch the news for any recent developments on the national front, but I have more immediate decisions to make. I want some better committee assignments, but that will depend on which party I decide to caucus with," Velvet sighed.

"You mean you would consider joining the Republican Party?" Wenonah exclaimed. "You ran as a Democrat, Joe ran as a Democrat, and the Republicans have given you the cold shoulder for years. They are not even in the same orbit as you on issues like tribal gaming and the environment."

"I know, but the Republicans will again control the new Congress and the legislative agenda for the next two years. If I caucus with them, I might have a chance of passing legislation and getting on a decent committee assignment where I can make a difference for my district. Otherwise, I am stuck with the minority Democrats again and face another two years in the political wilderness."

"Velvet, what are you thinking? The Republicans won't need you and will see you as a liability if this sex scandal thing doesn't go away. Where are your Democratic party principles?"

"I guess they died in August when I was blindsided by my party."

Wenonah cringed but understood. Probably a good play from a strategic standpoint, she mused, but not from her partisan perspective.

Velvet phoned Amy and asked her to assemble the staff that afternoon. She wanted a legislative priority list prepared before she bartered for specific committee assignments.

In the meantime, she began to think about the previously unthinkable: reassessing her continued loyalty to the Democratic Party.

* * *

Velvet's afternoon staff meeting had just gotten underway in her hotel room when a young volunteer burst into the room.

"Congresswoman, there is big news on the Maine Congressional race!"

The entire staff rushed to the television in the next room in time to see a banner run across the CNN news screen:

"BREAKING NEWS: MAINE SECRETARY OF STATE TO ANNOUNCE RESULTS OF SECOND CONGRESSIONAL DISTRICT RECOUNT"

Cameras panned a crowded press conference room in the state capitol.

The Maine Secretary of State walked up to a podium with dozens of microphones attached, blocking out all but his eyes and bald forehead. He then delivered his news in a very somber tone. "As you know, we began a recount shortly after midnight, recognizing the importance of the votes in the Second Congressional District. We mobilized every state resource available in a round-the-clock effort to complete the recount expeditiously."

You could hear a pin drop in the press conference as everyone waited eagerly for his findings.

"After consulting with state and local election officials, a recount of the initial vote tally confirms that the independent presidential candidate indeed has won the Second District popular vote and thus earned one electoral vote. We can also confirm that the outcome of the statewide popular vote is not significantly different from the earlier announced results."

Velvet watched as some reporters dashed from the room to spread the news. The Secretary paused and asked for calm as he offered the official pronouncement everyone was waiting for.

"Thus, I will soon certify that Maine will award one electoral vote for the independent candidate in the Second District, one electoral vote in the First Congressional District for the Democratic Party nominee, and two at-large votes for the Republican Party nominee based on her winning the overall statewide vote."

The electoral vote allocation for Maine remained unchanged.

The reporters shouted a flurry of questions at the Secretary. But Velvet instead turned to Wenonah with the key question: "Now what? Will the Presidential election go to the House since no one received the necessary 270 electoral votes, and will I be voting for the next President?"

"Not yet," Wenonah replied. "Just because Maine's electoral votes remain unchanged does not automatically throw the election to the House. There could be recounts in other states where the Presidential election was very close, or there could be some unfaithful electors."

"Unfaithful electors?" Velvet asked.

"Yes, despite a 2021 U.S. Supreme Court ruling allowing states to punish or even replace electors who cast electoral ballots for candidates other than the ones they pledged to vote for, it is still possible that electors in some states could switch their support to another candidate—and all it takes is one unfaithful elector to change the outcome of the Presidential election," Wenonah explained.

"So, an elector from a state that voted for the Democratic candidate can just change her mind and vote for the Republican and the election is over?" Velvet asked incredulously.

"Or vice versa. A couple of electors from a state that voted Republican could switch to the Democratic candidate and give the White House to the Dems. Or the lumberjack candidate could announce his support for the Republican and give her the Presidency," Wenonah continued.

"So, are electors just free to vote for whomever they want?"

"Well," Wenonah replied, "electors are reliable party faithful, but the consequences of the shift of a single elector's vote and likely private inducements by the opposing parties make the outcome of this electoral college vote more uncertain than at any other time in history."

"Unbelievable!" Velvet exclaimed.

"As we speak," Wenonah continued, "professionals from both parties are scrutinizing the slates of these otherwise faceless electors to determine who might be their weakest links, the so-called faithless electors."

Velvet was now seeing the dark underbelly of the electoral college process and was both appalled and intrigued by the political web Wenonah was spinning.

"Tell me more, Wenonah!"

"Each party will have two primary objectives," Wenonah began. "First, ensure that all their party's electors remain committed to vote for their party's nominee, and second, identify and pressure any electors in the other party's slate who might be tempted to switch sides for the right offer."

The seemingly endless political games yet to be played at the Presidential level were disturbing to Velvet, as she was still reeling from her unexpected political rebirth and an unfolding sex scandal in her campaign. But she realized she was seeing history in the making and pressed on.

"So why don't the Republicans just get the lumberjack candidate to throw his support to the Republican candidate and end this game?" Velvet asked.

"You have hit the nail on the head and answered your earlier question at the same time. That is why Maine is so important and why the lumberjack candidate is the key to this election," Wenonah smiled.

Wenonah, seeing the puzzled sister's face, stopped her political lecture and quizzed her sister.

"I am curious, Velvet. What would you do if you were the lumberjack candidate? Would you vote for the Republican candidate and provide her with the 270th vote needed to be President, or would you side with the Democrat and create a 269-269 tie and throw the election to the House of Representatives?"

Velvet paused, realizing the enormous political ramifications of the lumberjack's decision.

"I guess it would depend on what my goal was. Do I want the political power of a Presidential king maker, or do I want to pick the better Presidential candidate regardless of the politics of the situation? I think my duty would be to pick the best President, but I must admit it would be tempting to bargain for my vote. There are so many things I want to do for my district, but right now I have nothing to offer that anyone wants or needs."

"Now you understand the dilemma that many politicians face when they must choose between standing firm on their principles versus the political realities of governing," Wenonah responded. "Compromises are essential for government to work."

Velvet gazed at her sister and nodded that she understood.

"So, I guess we have to wait and see what the lumberjack candidate feels is more important," Velvet concluded.

"Yep," Wenonah replied.

* * *

Washington was awash with rumors of offers made to the lumberjack candidate by both parties, including agency posts, ambassadorships, party posts, and even key committee assignments for his newly elected son. Potential private sector jobs and university presidencies in his home state of Maine also were floated in local press stories.

Speculation in the media was that the lumberjack candidate would cast his electoral ballot for the Republican Presidential candidate since she had won the total popular vote in Maine; or, perhaps more personally, so the Republicans would offer his son an attractive committee assignment as a member of the majority party in the House.

But the lumberjack candidate kept his cards close to his chest, refusing to announce his decision before consulting his allies and supporters.

In the two weeks following the November election, the lumberjack candidate set up high-profile meetings with both party presidential nominees and with Congressional leaders of both parties to discuss how he might vote. He then scheduled a series of town hall meetings over a one-week period to listen to how his fellow Mainers felt he should vote.

Velvet marveled at the lumberjack's strategy, keeping the spotlight on himself by not tipping his hand on where he was leaning.

Thus, when the lumberjack candidate scheduled a press conference on December 1 at the state capitol to announce his decision, the press traveled in droves to Augusta.

Velvet and her key staff members were meeting at her home in Christmas developing their legislative strategy the day of the press conference. The television in the room was tuned to CNN but muted, though everyone had one eye on the screen for news of when the press conference would begin. When the regularly scheduled news program abruptly shifted to an Augusta hotel conference room filled with reporters, Velvet stopped the staff meeting and turned up the television volume.

"Let's see what the lumberjack decided after his prolonged decision-making process," Velvet declared.

The elevated podium in the room was so jammed with microphones that it resembled a cell phone tower. With such broad nationwide coverage, Velvet wondered wistfully what it must feel like to be at the height of political power and have the entire nation awaiting your next words?

Soon, the lumberjack candidate entered the room, accompanied by his wife, son, and a granddaughter who was confined to a wheelchair. The candidate looked tired but upbeat and his wife looked exhausted, though forcing a pained smile. His son was more subdued, and his granddaughter sat slumped forward in her wheelchair, oblivious to the throng of press before her.

The mixed family image on the television screen made what the lumberjack candidate was likely to say even more unpredictable.

"I think I would be a lot more excited than he seems to be," Velvet remarked.

After the lumberjack candidate introduced his family, thanked his supporters, and acknowledged his two major party opponents, he announced he would take no questions after his statement.

"I ran a protest campaign against the two major party candidates because they offered no new vision for our country; just a continuation of the same tired politics that for decades has failed us as a state and as a nation."

Velvet watched Wenonah's jaw tighten as his criticism of the parties heightened the tension in the room. "The voters of the Second Congressional District of Maine chose me over the other two major presidential candidates because I offered them an alternative to the status quo. They despised the swamp in Washington and chose me as a lumberjack to clear-cut it."

Silence permeated both Velvet's home and the press conference room as he cleared his throat to utter the words they had been waiting to hear. "For me to vote for either of the two major party candidates would be a betrayal of my pledge to the people of my state and to the nation. So, I will cast my one electoral ballot for myself when the electoral college voting takes place on December 16."

Reporters shouted a barrage of questions at the candidate; but only one reporter's question caught his attention as he was leaving the podium.

"So who do you think should become President?" the reporter asked.

The lumberjack candidate turned to the throng of reporters, smiling as he gave his response: "If my decision results in the inability of either major party candidate to reach the magical 270 electoral votes and instead throws the decision to the House of Representatives, I will present myself as the compromise candidate, should partisanship present a barrier to picking either of the other two."

He then exited with his family.

Reporters screamed other questions, but to no avail.

"Wow!" exclaimed Wenonah. "He really has a big ego if he thinks House members of either party will abandon their nominee for him. I can't believe he passed up what must have been some tremendous job offers and political support for his son just to feed his own ego."

"I disagree!" Velvet replied. "That took guts. There was principle in what he said as well as ego. But now that he has lost his bargaining power and foiled a quick resolution of the electoral college counting, where do we go?" Velvet asked.

"Well, if no elector flips, we still have a projected 269–268–1 electoral vote and may well have the first House election of a President in 200 years," Wenonah responded. "But we still have to wait to see if all the electors remain faithful when they vote on December 16."

"And we are really still in limbo until Congress actually counts the electoral college votes on January 6, right?"

"Yep," said Wenonah.

"I can't believe we still haven't picked a President. And I also can't believe that it might be Congress and not the voters or even the electors who will decide who are next President will be," Velvet responded in wonderment.

* * *

Velvet's staff continued chattering about the implications of the CNN news report for several minutes before Velvet decided she had heard enough about the electoral college process. To get their attention, Velvet turned off the television.

"Enough of this presidential circus for now. Let's focus our energy on what got us here and what I can do in Congress. Let's identify the most important issues we need to address for my district."

The staff members returned to their seats, awaiting her guidance.

"First, let's look at the barrels issue."

"Tom, get me more information about the Corps of Engineers dumping in Lake Superior, and let's determine where the missing barrels from the Marquette beach might be. Start digging," Velvet urged.

"Amy, Wenonah, and Taylor, I need you to contact my key supporters and ask them for their legislative priorities. That will help me decide what committees I should request in order to get legislation through the House."

Velvet smiled as they left her hotel room to take on their assignments.

While awaiting her staff's findings, Velvet weighed her most difficult decision. With which party should she caucus to achieve her legislative priorities? She had thought the choice was between principle and practical politics. But it now appeared they were not mutually exclusive considerations.

However, her political party choice had to be deferred again as other issues arose, demanding her immediate attention.

Tom reported back first and delivered the bad news about pressing the Corps for information about the barrels. Corps officials refused to offer further information. They argued that this issue might become the subject of a future litigation and directed him to the White House for further information.

"OK, I'll call the White House right now," Velvet responded.

Velvet placed a call to the White House Chief of Staff, seeking to override the Corps' resistance. But the Presidential election was all-consuming for the White House staff and her inquiry fell on deaf ears. An aide to the Chief of Staff called back and said they might have to defer her inquiry until a new Administration took office because of the Presidential election stand-off.

"Damn," Velvet fumed.

Amy called a few hours later and reported that, based on the legislative priorities of key supporters they contacted, Velvet should seek appointment to the House Committees on Natural Resources and Appropriations—the former having jurisdiction over tribal and environmental concerns and the latter would fund any of the projects she might propose.

"OK, now we're getting somewhere," Velvet happily declared.

Based on the staff recommendations, Velvet put feelers out to the House leaders of both parties about joining their respective caucuses.

The responses she received from her calls to party leaders were polite but noncommittal. She simply had no bargaining chip to negotiate with.

Stymied in her efforts to improve her legislative position, Velvet turned her attention to internal office organization and staffing issues, including appointing Amy as her permanent Administrative Assistant, Angela as her new press secretary, and Taylor as her new field coordinator.

I may not be a player yet, but at least I will be in a better position to navigate the legislative process after the Presidential battle is over by putting my house in order, she decided.

* * *

As it grew closer to the December 16 electoral college vote, rumors of faithless electors abounded, with stories about electors being offered posts in a new Administration or high-paying jobs in the private sector. However, there also was enormous party counterpressure on the electors.

In the last days preceding electoral college balloting, both parties warned of severe retribution for any disloyalty among their electors, while simultaneously seeking to lure away at least one or two faithless electors pledged to the opposing party's candidate.

Rumors of attempted elector defections continued but were unconfirmed.

But after the electoral college balloting in the various state capitols was completed, there were no other reported defections. So, it was assumed by top party professionals that when Congress and the Vice President opened the sealed ballots of all fifty states and the District of Columbia on January 6, neither party's candidate would receive the necessary 270 electoral votes.

Wenonah called Velvet on the evening of the December 16 electoral balloting with a cynical but constructive comment. "I think you, as an independent, will get a more positive response to your committee assignment requests and to White House inquiries now that the House likely has become the new 'decider.' Expect return phone calls soon, with both parties and the White House singing a different tune."

It was not long after Wenonah's call that Velvet's phone began ringing.

CHAPTER FOURTEEN

The House Rules

*"I used to like the idea of the popular vote, but now realize
the electoral college is far better for the U.S.A."*

—Former President Donald Trump

**MOUNT PLEASANT, MICHIGAN
MID-DECEMBER 2024**

THE TWO LOCAL REPORTERS WHO HAD REPORTED THE ALLEGED LEBLANC
campaign sex scandal sought a new angle on their story to compete with the
daily Presidential election headlines. They explored the constitutionally
mandated next steps if the electoral college could not produce a Presidential winner. Consulting a political scientist professor at Lake Superior State
University in the Soo, they learned that the Constitution empowers the House
of Representatives to select the next President under an unusual process.

Each state delegation, regardless of size, would have only one vote, determined by a majority vote of each state's Congressional delegation. The candidate who wins 26 states wins the Presidency. Michigan in 2024 had fifteen members of Congress, as it had lost a seat after the 2020 census: seven Republicans, seven Democrats and Velvet as an independent.

"Congresswoman LeBlanc may hold the tie-breaking vote that will determine how Michigan votes for President," the professor advised.

Surprised by that possibility, the reporters rushed to seek an appointment with Velvet.

However, after publication of their sex scandal story, Amy immediately rebuffed their request. They had burned any bridge to Velvet with their exposé.

Other reporters also recognized Velvet's new prominence. They too saw the possibility that Velvet's vote could be among the most consequential cast in the House now that the Maine election apparently was settled. Based on the current partisan make-up of the House, Michigan could become the necessary twenty-sixth state to decide who went to the White House.

Velvet's sudden popularity in the media caught both her and her staff off-guard. Local and national political reporters alike began flooding Amy with questions about who Velvet would support in case of a House vote.

"Amy, can you buy me some time? I want to think this through before making any commitments," Velvet quipped, remembering the delayed announcement strategy of the lumberjack candidate.

Amy begged them off as best she could, but the press was relentless.

Impatient for an answer, some state and national investigative reporters gamed Velvet's decision-making. They researched her past statements and actions to project her vote. How did her past policy positions line up with the positions of the two major party presidential candidates? The consensus among reporters was that she would support the Democratic candidate unless Republican offers lured her away.

Other reporters questioned members of Velvet's campaign staff for clues. They also began digging for more personal information about Velvet, whom they had ignored during her short stint in Washington and subsequent write-in candidacy in the general election. She was still an unknown political commodity except in the local media.

Recognizing her media fame was fleeting, Velvet set up a Zoom meeting with Wenonah and Frank to explore ways to take advantage of her newly found prominence.

I bet this is the power rush the lumberjack candidate felt only a few weeks ago at his press conference, Velvet chuckled to herself.

When the Zoom meeting began, Velvet tossed out the opening salvo.

"I think I just got the bargaining chip I need to help my district. What's my best course of action? How should I play my cards before disclosing who I support for President?"

Both Frank and Wenonah advised her to avoid tipping her hand as long as possible and wait for both political parties to make overtures to her.

"The longer you remain noncommittal about your party and candidate preference, the better the offers will become," Wenonah advised.

Velvet agreed that silence was the best policy as the electoral college issue dragged on. She already had a shaky relationship with the press, so she felt the best way to avoid tipping her hand and not further alienating them was to avoid direct encounters altogether. So, when Amy gave Velvet a long list of national media figures seeking an "exclusive interview" with her, Velvet asked Amy to delay replying to all of them.

Instead, taking Tom's advice, she asked Amy to set up a private meeting with a well-connected American University political science professor to discuss the mechanics of the U. S House of Representatives Presidential selection process and her strategic options.

The meeting was scheduled for December 19 at her home in Christmas, but the press had planted television crews near her front yard waiting for her arrival. Instead, Taylor drove Velvet to the Soaring Eagle Casino and Resort in Mount Pleasant, as the press would assume her alternative venue would be the nearby Soo Kewadin casino, 200 miles north of Mount Pleasant.

Velvet reserved a block of rooms at the Soaring Eagle hotel under an assumed name. The Saginaw Chippewa tribe was more than happy to provide her with the privacy she needed to make what could be the most consequential political decision of her life.

Tom, the professor, and Wenonah had already arrived from the nearby Midland Airport. Meeting over coffee in her hotel suite that evening, the group took notes as the professor unwrapped the likely House election scenarios if the decision fell to the House.

The professor began by discussing the scant history of the House handling a presidential selection process. He explained the few major rules governing the process and the tough task facing the Speaker to control the politics of that process.

Then, the professor described the likely partisan drama that would unfold if the House indeed were to conduct a vote.

He began with the known facts. The 2025 House would have twenty-five red states, where a majority of the Congressional members of each state's delegation were Republicans. These twenty-five states would certainly support the Republican nominee.

There were twenty-two states that were blue states where a majority of the Congressional members of each state's delegation were Democrats. They would certainly vote for the Democratic nominee.

That left only three states where the votes were uncertain: Maine, Michigan, and Vermont.

Maine was a wildcard, the professor added, but the lumberjack's son telegraphed that as the new congressman he would vote for his father on the first ballot. So, since Maine has only two members of Congress, the vote would be a 1–0–1.

"It would require both members to vote for the same candidate to achieve a majority in Maine," Tom interjected.

Wenonah jumped in at the mention of Vermont, which had an independent member elected to its single Congressional district. The independent member had signaled early support for the Democratic nominee, she reported. Thus, the Democrats should have twenty-three votes, but would still be three votes short of the twenty-six votes needed.

"Then there's Michigan, which has fifteen members—seven Republicans, seven Democrats, and you," Wenonah concluded, smiling at Velvet.

There was a dramatic pause as Wenonah's comment sank in.

Then the professor continued his presentation.

"If we project twenty-five state votes for the Republican and twenty-three for the Democrat, the Democratic candidate can't win the Presidency even with Michigan's vote."

There was a long pause before the professor nodded at Velvet and continued.

"But the Republican nominee also can't win without it."

Velvet's face flushed.

"The eyes of the political world will soon turn to Michigan and the decision of its independent member of Congress," he predicted.

"So, if Maine remains deadlocked, Michigan becomes the new epicenter of the Presidential elections, right?" Velvet concluded.

"That's right," said the professor. "Welcome to the maelstrom of political maneuvering on the road to the White House."

Velvet paused, realizing the precarious political situation he had just described.

"Putting aside my personal preference for the President," she said, looking at everyone in the room," how do you think I can best leverage my position as an Independent?"

Thus, began a round robin discussion of options and recommendations, along with a few pointed but unsuccessful probes to discover where Velvet was leaning personally.

After nearly twenty minutes of pro-con discussion, Velvet temporarily adjourned the meeting. "I need time to absorb all this information. Let me make a few calls and we'll reconvene tomorrow morning."

As the small group left, Velvet checked her phone to see if she had received any important messages during their meeting.

She had.

Amy had called four times in the past hour.

Did Amy's repeated calls mean trouble ahead?

She reached for a bottle of water and sat at the hotel room desk, bracing for bad news. Then, after taking a deep gulp, she returned Amy's call.

Amy blurted out that there had been a flurry of calls to her Washington and district offices.

Wenonah was right about a newfound interest in returning her phone calls, Velvet thought.

"Tell me who called?"

"Well, the White House Chief of Staff called about your Corps of Engineers issue, the Speaker and Minority Leader about your committee assignment requests, the Republican Vice-Presidential candidate—"

"Wait, what?" Velvet interrupted angrily. "That low life," she interjected.

Amy continued, "the Governor, Connie, the Michigan Democratic Party Chair—"

"Connie, you've got to be kidding!" Velvet exclaimed in disgust.

"And a score of press invitations, including all three major networks, CNN, Fox, and even The Rachel Maddow Show."

"Rachel Maddow!" Velvet playfully shouted. "I love her."

But then she came down to earth, remembering the fate of the lumberjack candidate after he telegraphed his decision to the press and lost his political advantage. Reluctantly, she instructed Amy to decline all media invitations.

"Any thoughts on who I will not call on that list?" she teased.

Amy replied, "I think I know."

"I think it's time to call the White House again. Would you join me in a conference call I will make in a few minutes?" Velvet asked.

Amy agreed, and Velvet hung up.

Velvet texted Tom and asked him to arrange a White House conference call that would include Amy, the professor, Wenonah, and himself.

Tom promptly arrived with the professor and Wenonah and began making arrangements for the White House conference call.

"Tom, text Taylor to come here as well. I think he is downstairs meeting with his student friends. Then put the White House call through and see if we can get the barrel issue back on this Administration's agenda," Velvet directed.

While Tom was texting Taylor, the professor excused himself, as he was not familiar with the barrel issue and felt his presence was not needed.

Velvet and Wenonah thanked him for his presentation, and then turned to the White House call just as Taylor arrived.

The four sat together on the hotel couch, with Amy listening by phone in Washington. Tom hooked up the speakerphone and placed the call to the White House Chief of Staff. The call from Velvet went directly to the Chief of Staff himself.

"That's a switch," Velvet whispered, having had her previous calls screened by his aides.

After thanking Velvet for returning his call, the Chief of Staff apologized for the delay in responding to the Corps issue. He insisted the staff person who took her prior message forgot to forward Velvet's message to him until that morning.

"The President is deeply concerned about the dumping issue and has ordered the Corps to investigate and report back to him directly. The investigation will begin immediately," he continued. "We will notify you of their findings after they brief the President."

But Velvet would not be brushed aside with his vague assurances and pressed him further.

"Why did the White House stop the EPA from examining the contents of the second wave of barrels? And why has your office brushed off all my previous inquiries about this issue?" Velvet asked skeptically.

After a rambling and evasive response, the Chief of Staff said he would investigate her past unanswered inquiries and that "heads would roll." He added in a hushed tone that there were national security issues about the barrels that he couldn't discuss over the phone.

National security issues, thought Velvet? Really? Or was this just an excuse to cover up a scandal? But she did not vocalize her skepticism of what she felt was a red herring issue. There would be a better time to broach this issue.

Then he offered her the opportunity to co-chair a presidential task force the President proposed to create after the investigation if any clean-up was deemed necessary. He assured her there would be ample resources—both agency personnel and funding—to address any recommended remediation; and that the President would earmark resources in the Corps budget for this purpose before he left office.

He also informed her that the President had a previous conversation with the Republican Presidential nominee and felt she would support the President's task force proposal.

The investigation and a follow-up task force pleased Velvet.

"This all depends on who controls the White House next month, of course."

There it was. The sly but not unexpected lobbying underlying the White House offer.

Wenonah pointed to her watch and signaled with her lips for Velvet to ask for a timeline for these decisions, and Velvet pressed further.

"How long will the Corps investigation take? Would a preliminary report be available before a new Administration is in place?" she pressed. "And what guarantee do I have that I would co-chair the subsequent task force?"

Again, the Chief of Staff gave an evasive response, reiterating that the President wanted a thorough investigation which might not be completed before his term expired. But he believed the Republican nominee would honor the task force chair commitment.

After thanking him and ending the call, she asked, "Well, what do you all think?"

Tom and Wenonah chimed in, "Get it in writing!"

Velvet agreed and asked Tom to compose a letter to the Chief of Staff, summarizing the conversation and asking him to confirm her understanding of the President's offer for an investigation and her co-chairing a task force.

"Finally, something of political significance is happening because of me," she smiled with satisfaction.

She then moved down her list of callers. This was a time in her political journey when anything seemed possible.

So, this is the lofty feeling of political power that so many crave, she thought.

Having concluded her conversation with the White House, Velvet wondered what her newly found power could do to enhance her clout in the House in January, no matter who was elected President.

Wenonah suggested the next person for Velvet to call should be the Speaker of the House, the most powerful leader in the chamber she would soon rejoin.

Velvet agreed.

Tom placed the call to the Speaker's office. Rather than being told the Speaker was busy and to leave a message as had been the case in past calls, Velvet's call went directly to the Speaker.

After exchanging pleasantries, the Speaker said he had talked with his Republican leadership team and that they wanted Velvet to join their caucus. "I was told you are interested in serving on two major committees, Appropriations and Natural Resources. Those are two mighty important committees and I have a long list of Republican members who want on one or both. But if you caucus with us, I will do my level best to get you on at least one of these committees."

Velvet thanked him for his promised efforts and recognized that half a loaf was better than nothing. But she pressed for another commitment.

"I spoke with the White House about the Corps issue and was told the President has promised to investigate the Corps dumping. If warranted, would you support the subsequent formation of a task force to pursue any of its recommendations and for me to serve as co-chair?"

Her directness surprised the Speaker, but he clearly was aware of the White House offer. He promised to meet with White House officials soon, assuring her he was close to the President and was sure he could support the Chief of Staff's proposal.

Then, the Speaker added one last sweetener to the conversation. He claimed he had known Joe well and thought highly of him. He repeated his condolences for her loss and congratulated her on holding onto his seat. Knowing her dislike of the former Republican incumbent whom both she and Joe had now defeated, he pledged that neither he nor the RNC would endorse nor financially support any new effort by that former incumbent Republican Congressman to run against her in 2026, should she choose to seek re-election.

The Speaker then added dryly, "That is, if a Republican is in the White House in 2025."

Velvet finished with some personal inquiries about the Speaker's family before ending the conversation.

Wow, she thought, the Republicans have put a lot on the table.

* * *

After her conversation with the Speaker was over, Velvet wondered whether to just throw in with the Republicans. What could the Dems offer me that would top that?

But just then, her phone rang. The caller ID said Michigan Democratic Party, but she did not recognize the number. Out of curiosity, she answered it.

"Hello?"

"Hi Velvet, it's Connie."

Ugh, she thought. The last person in the world I want to talk to. But she had no choice but to continue with the call.

"Hello, Connie," Velvet said coolly. "What can I do for you?"

After offering belated congratulations for Velvet's victory, Connie said she was calling to invite Velvet back to the Democratic family. She reminded Velvet that both Joe and she shared the values of the Democratic Party and hoped she would rejoin the caucus.

To give the Republicans control of the White House and both Houses of Congress, Connie cautioned, would "eviscerate the policies we value as Democrats. We saw what happened when the Republicans controlled both branches of government in 2017, and we can't let that happen again," Connie warned.

Connie's words had little impact on Velvet. The hurtful stories of her alleged affair with Joe and the long delay in making a congratulatory call were infuriating.

The tone and hesitation in Connie's voice as she casually dismissed Joe's sex scandal as a "big lie" reinforced her suspicion that stories of Joe's affair with Connie were true.

Connie continued her spiel about the value of Velvet joining the Democratic caucus and, by implication, supporting the Democratic nominee for President.

She also claimed to speak for key Democratic party leaders who promised to give Velvet some prime committee assignments, strong campaign financing for her re-election, and not to support any primary opponents in subsequent elections if she joined the Democratic caucus. And if she wanted a high-level post in a new Democratic administration, that too could be arranged.

"And what about the Corps investigation?" Velvet interrupted.

Connie explained she talked with top party leaders and promised Democrats would push for a full investigation of the barrel dumping issue if they controlled the White House. Essentially, the sky was the limit in return for Velvet's vote and her fidelity to the Democratic party.

As exciting as these offers were, Velvet found Connie's promises and entreaties hollow and unpersuasive, as the hypocrisy of Connie pleading for fidelity repulsed her.

"And maybe Jim Zenger can rejoin your staff. He would be a good conduit between the party and your office," Connie suggested.

Why is she bringing up Jim, Velvet thought?

Then, she recalled her last conversation with Jim when he referred to Taylor as "lover boy".

Suddenly, it dawned on her. Of course, Jim was the leak! How did she miss that?

"Hello, Velvet, are you still there?" Connie asked, as Velvet was not responding to her suggestion.

"Yes, I'm here. Just give me a minute."

Well, at least now I know that neither Taylor nor Amy was not the source of the scandalous headlines, she thought.

"Anything else, Connie?"

After impatiently listening to Connie drone on for several more minutes, Velvet told her she had other calls to return and cut off their conversation.

Her preference all along, though she disclosed it to no one, was to support the Democratic Presidential nominee. But maybe the Democratic Party was not where she should be since she was so contemptuous of the state party chair.

However, siding with the Republican nominee did not sit well with her from a policy standpoint.

Velvet looked further down her list of return calls and saw the name of another unwelcome caller: the Republican Vice-Presidential nominee.

"Wenonah, why would the Republican nominee for Veep call me, especially because of his previous hostility towards me, my campaign, and to minorities?" Velvet asked.

"I had the same question when I heard about the call-back list, so I texted Tom's professor friend. He replied by texting me the Twelfth Amendment."

She then handed Velvet her cell phone with a highlighted part of the amendment:

Amendment XII: And if the House of Representatives shall not choose a President whenever the right of choice shall devolve upon them … then the Vice-President shall act as President, as in the case of the death or other constitutional disability of the President.

"Boil this down for me, Wenonah," Velvet pleaded. "How does this explain his call to me?"

"Well," Wenonah explained, "if the House cannot find twenty-six states to support a presidential nominee, the newly elected vice president selected by the Senate would serve as Acting President. Since Republicans will control the Senate in the new Congress, it's likely that the Senate will approve the Republican vice-presidential nominee, who then would assume the Presidency until the House reaches the twenty-six–state vote threshold."

Velvet rolled her eyes. She had grudging respect for the Republican Presidential nominee with whom she shared some important social policy positions. However, she loathed her running mate, who had campaigned for her Republican opponent in the general election and directed significant donations to him from his own PAC.

As much as Velvet disliked him, she was curious about his pitch as she mulled over the idea of supporting the Republican nominee. So, she called him back and put his call on speaker.

He answered the phone and got right to the point.

"Evangeline. I know you and I don't see eye to eye on many issues, but I wanted to make sure you understand the consequences of voting with the Democratic members of the Michigan Congressional delegation. The House could not deliver the vital twenty-sixth vote to elect the next President."

"Yes, I know this," Velvet responded.

He continued, "I expect the Senate will confirm me as Vice President. Until they find twenty-six votes, I become the Acting President. What do you think of that?"

"You are a danger to the environment, a bigot, and someone who backed my Republican Congressional opponent whom Joe and I strongly opposed. That's what I think of that," she responded in an uncharacteristically caustic tone.

"Well, I disagree with your first two accusations, but it's true that I supported Jack in the general. He and I go way back, and I supported him for personal reasons and not because I had anything against you or Joe—other than you were both Democrats!" he chuckled. "In fact, I am impressed by how resilient you've been. My compliments for winning the hard way by a write-in campaign."

Velvet did not respond, so he continued.

"But let me get to the heart of the matter. My running mate doesn't know, nor would she condone, my calling you; but I'm calling you, anyway. I know they put me on the ticket with her to placate the conservative wing of my party, and I know I'll be relegated to funerals and parades with no actual power under my running mate."

Then he delivered his most powerful argument. "But if you vote against my Republican running mate just because you don't like me and the House is unable to elect a President, the Senate will make me the acting President, *comprende?*"

Velvet remained silent.

He continued, "So a vote for the Democrat Presidential nominee is cutting off your nose to spite your face. Vote for my Republican running mate and you make me powerless. Vote for the Democrat and give me the power of an acting President, even if it is just for a few days."

"Thank you for that grim calculation," Velvet responded.

"Evangeline, there is too much at stake to leave this presidential election decision hanging any longer. You can end this perilous process only by voting for my running mate."

"Thank you for that analysis. Now if you will excuse me, I have more calls to make before I make such a decision." and she broke off the call.

Wenonah and Tom were as startled by the candor of the Republican Vice-Presidential nominee as Velvet was.

"Enough posturing for the time being. I need to get out of here for a while. You guys get some sleep, as I'll need you both fresh when we meet first thing tomorrow morning."

* * *

Velvet left her hotel room to clear her head. She headed down to the casino floor. Some mindless wandering was in order. Despite her frequent visits to the Soo casino to meet with Frank, she had never set foot on a casino gaming floor before and wondered what the attraction was to gamble.

It surprised her to see so many people stuffing money into noisy slot machines, mainly senior citizens. They were playing a game where eventually the house wins—kind of like her playing in the realm of politics against the political establishment. But there is always that slim hope that you are the one to beat the odds.

She saw a disheveled, white-haired woman sitting at a slot machine and wearing an oxygen mask to help her breathe in the crowded casino floor. She watched as the woman mechanically inserted more and more bills into the machine, more than her external appearance would seem prudent.

Velvet wanted to learn more about this gambling attraction to take her mind off her political dilemma, so she walked over to where the woman was sitting and sat down at the slot machine next to her.

It was apparent that Velvet didn't know how to play the slots, and an awkward silence occurred as Velvet tried reading the instructions on the machine.

Since the woman showed no interest in Velvet's floundering, Velvet tried to engage her differently.

"Hi, I'm Velvet. This is my first time on a casino floor, but you probably guessed that already. Are you from around here, and do you come here often?"

The woman was oblivious to her inquiries and refused to remove her oxygen mask to speak. In fact, after Velvet made several more unsuccessful inquiries, the woman turned towards her and gave her an annoyed look before resuming her mechanical punching of the slot machine button.

"I'm sorry to bother you, but I don't know how to insert a $10 bill into this machine."

The elderly woman took off her mask and snapped the bill from Velvet's hand, putting it in the paper slot of the machine.

"Push that button," she snapped, pointing to the maximum bet button. Then she put her mask back on and turned back to her own machine.

It turned out Velvet was playing a quarter slot machine and her maximum bet would cost her $2.25 for each play. She pushed the bet button as instructed but did not win on her first attempt. It was clear the woman next to her was not interested in further engagement, so Velvet made one more bet. But pressing the maximum button a second time, she hit three red sevens for a $240 win.

The woman next to her spit out an expletive, stood up, and left, muttering something, but Velvet only recognized the word "squaw."

Velvet felt a rush come over her to win so much on a $2.25 dollar bet. Was it really that easy, she wondered? She then played for another forty-five minutes, oblivious to anyone else on the floor. Soon she not only lost her $240 but also the original $10 she had inserted into the machine.

A lot like politics. The wins are few and far between, she thought. But the thrill of a win keeps you coming back for more.

Velvet left the casino floor but did not go back to her hotel room. Instead, she stopped at the lounge and its large, perpetually lit gas fireplace near the hotel front desk. Sitting on a brown leather couch, she watched the dancing flames in a semitrance. No one paid attention to a First American woman wearing a green headband and sitting on a couch in a tribal casino.

However, she still had calls to make, followed by a morning strategy meeting with Tom, Wenonah, Amy, and Taylor. She went to her hotel room to make one more call before turning in for the night.

It was an obligatory return call to the Governor.

Unfortunately, or fortunately from Velvet's standpoint, the Governor was not available when she called him. That was a win in her eyes, as she knew she had to return his call, but really didn't want to talk to him. By leaving a voice mail message on the phone of the Governor's receptionist, she satisfied that responsibility.

She then turned off her phone and fell onto her bed, closing her eyes. The world of politics could wait as she absorbed her new political prominence.

It felt like it had been only a few minutes before she heard a knock on her door. Looking at the clock, it was morning. She had slept through the night, and the knock meant her staff were ready for their morning meeting.

I should have canceled the meeting, she thought. With so many political unknowns remaining between now and Monday, January 6, 2025, the official electoral college ballot counting date, the meeting seems so unnecessary.

But it was too late now, so she invited them in.

"Sorry, I'm a bit disheveled," she said, referring to her rumpled clothes. "Long night. But go ahead and make your presentations."

Tom and Wenonah described the remaining escape routes in the constitutional process that might obviate the need for a House vote. There were rumors that there might be a successful challenge to one state's electoral ballots, which could resolve the Presidential election without a House vote. There also were rumors of some last-minute backroom bargains that were being made with small state delegation members, reminiscent of the Presidential backroom deals of the nineteenth century.

"OK. No sense in worrying about things out of my control," she concluded.

Then, smiling, she rose from her chair.

"Congress has adjourned for the Christmas holiday, so let's get out of here and let Washington sort this out. Go home and enjoy the Christmas holiday," Velvet instructed.

It was back to Christmas to enjoy the holiday season solo.

CHAPTER FIFTEEN

The House Votes

"I have not aligned myself with any party.
Sitting tight waiting for an attractive offer."

—Will Rogers

WHILE VELVET WAS BUSY MAKING TRAVEL PLANS, PARTY LEADERS HAD more immediate concerns.

The House leadership had thoroughly explored all plausible scenarios that would avoid a House vote. They predicted an inconclusive electoral college outcome on Monday, January 6, and set Tuesday, January 7 for a House vote to decide the Presidency. Both parties notified their members of this likelihood and instructed their members to return from the holiday break no later than Monday.

Velvet, who had been treated like a lame duck by the Democrats after her defeat in the August primary, had inadvertently been removed from the Democrat email roster and did not receive notice of an early return directive from the House leadership.

So, when she left for the holiday, she planned a peaceful and reflective vacation. She assumed that since the Speaker had agreed weeks earlier to a Tuesday, January 7 swear-in date; it was unlikely that the House would act on the Presidential election prior to that, if indeed a House vote was even needed after the final electoral college tally on January 6.

The thought of returning to her home in Christmas after her political rollercoaster ride over the past few days in Washington was a welcome respite before her planned return to the Capitol on Tuesday afternoon.

On New Year's Eve, she received a phone call from Tom reminding her of the special House vote scheduled for noon on Tuesday.

"Remind me?" she shouted. "Nobody told me about the date change. I already asked for and was given permission by the Speaker weeks ago to take my oath of office late Tuesday afternoon."

"Leadership said they emailed you about the January 6 return date over a week ago," Tom replied.

"What the heck!" she fumed. "I don't know if I can make it. Let me call you back, Tom."

Where to start, she mumbled to herself?

First, there was the transportation problem. She had purchased an expensive, nonrefundable, round-trip ticket with her return flight to Washington not arriving until late Tuesday afternoon, the day of the scheduled noon House vote. With her Congressional travel budget exhausted, she had paid for the flight with her own funds.

More important than the cost of changing tickets, she faced commercial flights in the Upper Peninsula that were infrequent, limited, and unpredictable this time of year. Thus, it would be extremely difficult to change the time of her return flight to Washington, now scheduled for 3 pm.

A quick call to the airport confirmed that there were no available flights prior to Tuesday and no seats available on the only other earlier departing flight earlier that day from the Soo.

With that, she texted Tom to contact the House leadership and advise them she could not attend the Monday House session. Instead, she would arrive Tuesday afternoon as previously planned to take her oath of office.

When Tom relayed the message to the offices of the Speaker and the Minority Leader, political professionals from both parties reacted swiftly. They were now convinced it would be the House and not the electoral college which would decide the Presidential election and that Michigan was a key state vote.

Her absence on the first day of voting triggered an avalanche of offers from both sides of the aisle to fly her by private plane to ensure her earlier arrival.

But most of the offers came with a catch: she would have to disclose for which presidential candidate she was going to vote; all except the Governor's office, who offered his personal jet without querying her voting preferences. His message was that he wanted to make sure Michigan had a voice in the Presidential election, as her absence would leave the Michigan delegation with a likely 7-7 tie.

When Tom told her of the Governor's offer, Velvet was not particularly pleased with the prospect. But the alternative transportation offers were even less desirable. She accepted his offer and said she would be ready to leave at 9 am on Tuesday out of the nearby Chippewa International Airport in Kinross. That would get her into Washington in time for the noon opening session of the House.

Tom advised her that the Governor's chief of staff would accompany her to Washington.

"I'm OK with that. At least I don't have to sit face to face with the Governor," she replied.

With that decided, Velvet called Taylor, who was still in Mount Pleasant packing his belongings and preparing to join Velvet in Washington. Velvet had promised him a position as her field staff coordinator, working out of Washington with frequent trips to the district accompanying Velvet. It would be much like Jim Zenger's role during Joe's term in Congress.

Would she travel from Mount Pleasant to Christmas on Sunday, January 5, she asked? Then they could drive together to the Soo Monday morning, when she could visit her spiritual family at the old Mission Hill Cemetery, meet with tribal officials, and chat with her field staff in the Soo. Along the way, she also wanted to talk to him about some ideas for office reorganization.

Without checking the weather, Taylor agreed to the plan.

Velvet called the Soo Kewadin Casino and reserved two hotel rooms for Monday night, so she and Taylor could catch the early morning flight on the Governor's plane the next day.

* * *

Taylor soon discovered he faced tough weather conditions if he were to drive to Christmas on Sunday. So, he booked a cheap commuter flight to the Soo from a nearby airport in Midland. As fate would have it, the airline lost his luggage, and he had to drive the campaign car from the Soo to Velvet's home in Christmas with only the clothes on his back.

It was a perilous drive from the Soo, as the icy roads to Christmas took him twice as long to navigate as it normally would. Even the press did not venture out on the roads to find Velvet because of the weather.

When he arrived at Velvet's home at dusk, she greeted him warmly. Velvet was happy to have some real physical company after days of holiday isolation. Taylor was the perfect companion for the next step in her political journey.

After a bite to eat and some brief political discussions, Taylor's eyes were drooping, and Velvet shooed him off to bed. Taylor did not object, as the thought of a warm shower and bed after a nail-biting winter ride was most appealing.

The next morning was a sunny one, with beams of light glistening off the newly fallen snow. Like the parking lot in the casino the morning after the November election day, all was white and pristine.

It's as though the slate of my past political trials has been wiped clean, and I've been given a new lease on my political life, Velvet fantasized as she gazed out her window.

After a quick breakfast, they began their journey east to the Soo.

On the way, Velvet had a steady stream of text messages from Wenonah and Amy.

Her first stop was at the old Mission Hill Cemetery.

"I will just be a few minutes, Taylor."

She knelt at her parent' monument, chanting an Ojibwe prayer and then made a solemn request:

"Mother and Father, please help me as I journey down the political path the Great Spirit has laid before me. I love you so."

After a few moments of silence, she rose refreshed, and returned to the car to continue her trip.

Upon her arrival in the Soo on Monday, Velvet wore a colorful blouse and her favorite red and green wrap-around skirt for her meeting with tribal leaders. I want to meet with my people in our clothing, not the clothes of the white establishment, she thought.

Next, she traveled to her Soo district office to meet with her staff. With Taylor at her side, she outlined her legislative agenda and some of the staffing decisions she would make upon taking her oath of office.

She then returned to the casino hotel to prepare for her trip to Washington the following morning.

However, a winter storm brewing over northern Lake Superior Monday morning had, by nightfall, approached the Michigan shoreline. Early Tuesday morning it unleashed its full fury on all roads leading to the Soo. All flights in and out of the Chippewa County International Airport in Kinross were canceled in anticipation of blizzard conditions.

The Governor's plane, leaving from the downstate capitol very early Tuesday morning, had to be diverted to the Pellston airport—at least a two-hour drive from the Kinross airport on a good day. The plane could get no closer,

Worse yet, the Kinross airport would not re-open until Wednesday, and icy road conditions in northern Michigan made the two-hour car drive to the Governor's plane in Pellston too dangerous to attempt.

"Gitche Gumee, what have you done?" she moaned. "Here, I am at a pivotal moment to protect you, and I am stranded in the Upper Peninsula. Am I going to become a political bystander again?"

"Everyone in Washington wants you there," Taylor responded. "Surely, there is someone else who can help us."

"You're right, Taylor. If I am a crucial vote on Tuesday, they will either delay the vote until I get there or help me get there in time," Velvet replied with a certain sense of optimism.

She called Tom and asked him to convey to the Speaker that not only would she be unable to take her oath of office on Tuesday afternoon as planned, but she also would miss the entire first day of the planned House vote on the Presidential election.

The Speaker did not respond to Tom's message about Velvet's delay right away.

He had more immediate issues to address.

* * *

The House leadership was frantically preparing for the Presidential House vote, as the electoral college votes were officially counted on Monday; and, as the experts had predicted, no one reached the 270-vote threshold. Hammering out the details of how the House would handle a vote that had not been undertaken in two centuries now was his top priority.

The Speaker recognized early on that there simply was no time to create a new process for the House vote. The Constitution provided only a bare outline of how the House was to make this decision. So, he pushed for adoption of the House rules used to decide the last Presidential contested election in 1824.

The sticking point back then was transparency. For the 1824 Presidential election, the most controversial issue in the rules was whether the House voting would be open to the public. The House decided then that the doors to the House chambers would be closed, and the galleries would be vacant.

That is what the Speaker wanted to have happen again for this election, as there would be a lot of wheeling and dealing that he felt would reflect poorly upon the selection process if open to press and public scrutiny. But he also knew there would be great pushback by the Democrats and some in his own party for such a closed-door rule, so it would be a close vote.

At noon on Tuesday, the House convened, and the Speaker ordered a roll call vote to ensure that at least two-thirds of the states were represented, one of the few constitutional requirements for the House process. Upon confirmation that the quorum requirement was met, the Speaker moved to the key procedural issue: the rules to guide this vote.

The Speaker pushed for a vote that the House would operate under the 1825 Rules for Presidential Elections. While there were many questions about this procedure, an outline of the steps had been emailed previously to all members. The debate focused then, as it did 200 years ago, on the closed nature of the process.

The Democrats argued how unfair it was not to allow the public and the press to watch the House voting process. After several tirades and procedural challenges by frustrated Democrats, the Speaker moved for adoption of the rules, which were approved largely on party lines.

Upon confirmation of a quorum and adoption of the 200-year-old House rules, the doors to the House chamber were closed, the galleries were cleared of all visitors, and the balloting proceeded.

Representatives of each state sat together on the House floor and each state voted along party lines for the candidate of their choice.

With the galleries empty, reporters had to rely on reports from House members and key House staff members passing in and out of the House chamber doors to monitor the results of the first ballot.

Members of the Michigan press corps called each member of their state's congressional delegation to get a read on the likely state vote. They received responses from fourteen of them, but the office of the fifteenth member, Velvet LeBlanc, did not respond.

When word came that the Governor's plane carrying Velvet was turned back due to weather, press headlines predicted Michigan would not be able to cast a vote for the President.

Reporters, reviewing the House procedures from the 1824 election which the Speaker had distributed, found under the Constitution that: "The House shall continue to ballot for a President, with no interruption by other business, until a President is elected." So, a long wait or even no decision by the House was possible, leaving it to whomever the Senate confirmed as Vice President to serve as the Acting President.

One Internet headline read: "Next President may be none of the above!"

With that possibility, the race was on to find out when Velvet would return to Washington and how she planned to vote.

* * *

Velvet spent Tuesday in her hotel room, making calls to Tom and her Washington office staff to keep abreast of the floor action while awaiting her Wednesday flight to Washington. On a call with Tom, she learned that the first House vote resulted in a 25–23 vote in favor of the Republican nominee as expected, with Maine and Michigan unable to deliver a majority vote from their delegations.

CNN had previously announced the independent member from Maine would not be voting for his father on the second ballot. The announcement, however, was anti-climactic. No matter how he voted, it would not decide the election. By voting for the Republican nominee, the other Democratic Congressman would cancel his vote and Maine still could not vote, as it would be a 1–1 tie. If he voted for the Democratic nominee, it would give the Democrats one more state but still leave the House vote in an indecisive 25–24 vote.

"So, where are we now?" Velvet asked.

"Well, we just completed a second balloting and it led to a 25–24 vote, with the Maine independent congressman voting with the other Democratic state delegation member and allowing Maine to cast its vote. But that still leaves the Republicans one vote shy of the necessary 26 votes and the Democrats need two."

"What do you think will happen now?" Velvet continued after digesting the second House vote.

"All the state delegations are now pretty firm in their partisan commitments, so all attention has now turned to Michigan, the only state that has not voted. If Michigan votes for the Republican, the election is over. If it votes for the Democrat, it would be a 25–25 tie. Until someone gets 26 state votes, the election is in limbo."

"OMG! What a nightmare!" Velvet exclaimed.

"The question everyone is asking is 'Where's Velvet?'" Tom added.

"Tell them I'm coming as fast as the weather permits. But I'm also hearing news reports of some strange happenings in the Senate. What's going on there?"

Tom advised her that the Senate had inexplicably deadlocked on the first balloting for the next Vice President. The Republican vice-presidential nominee had made many enemies in his own party by his outrageous statements and actions, reminding them of a candidate who had won the 2016 presidential election. Reluctant to re-live that turbulent time, two moderate Republican Senators abstained and the Senate's first vote to confirm the next vice president was a 49–49 tie.

The two Republican holdouts later declared on the Senate floor they would not change their minds. Tom explained that their decision to withhold support for their party's vice-presidential nominee had significant political consequences, citing the Twelfth Amendment wording that requires the Senate to confirm the Vice President by a majority vote.

With a tie and no immediate way to get to a majority vote since the Senate now had only a narrow 51–49 Republican advantage, the Senate adjourned and leaders of both parties raced to corral the necessary 51 votes to elect a Vice President.

"Is there any chance the Republican vice-presidential candidate could become President while we deliberate in the House?" Velvet asked.

"Right now, I would say no, as those two Republican Senators are pretty firm," Tom replied.

"That's a relief," Velvet muttered. "Thanks, and please keep me informed."

Then Wenonah called and began her conversation with the words: "You are now the hottest commodity in D.C."

"Wow!" Velvet shouted. "But to stay hot, I guess I have to stay silent. Isn't that ironic!"

After a brief conversation with Wenonah, she shut off her phone and turned to Taylor, who had been listening to her conversations.

"Taylor, please don't tell anyone where we are now—not Amy, not the Speaker, not anyone."

Taylor nodded in agreement.

"Maybe the storm from Lake Superior was a good thing after all," she mused out loud. "Gitche Gumee has maximized the value of my vote."

Taylor agreed but cautioned: "You know if someone else flips and the House picks the next President without you, you will lose all your leverage by holding out too long. There are several one-member states where if a single person is persuaded to flip, your vote would be unnecessary."

"I know, but I feel in my heart that I am on the path that the Great Spirit has planned for me. I'm gambling the House will stay deadlocked, as Wenonah told me everyone put all their cards on the table during the first ballot. It will be hard for anyone to change their vote now."

Taylor did not respond, still assessing the implications of her strategy.

"Don't you agree?" she asked Taylor.

He smiled, and then slowly nodded in agreement. It was a political gamble that could pay tremendous dividends—if it worked!

CHAPTER SIXTEEN

The President Is Calling

"Forgive your enemies, but never forget their names."

—John F. Kennedy

WASHINGTON. D.C.
TUESDAY JANUARY 7, 2025

AFTER TWO UNSUCCESSFUL HOUSE VOTES ON TUESDAY AND THE SENATE'S unsuccessful attempt to elect the new Vice President, the House recessed until Thursday. The Speaker knew this would be an intense time for negotiations among members of each state delegation and felt they needed an extra day to resolve the deadlock.

He spent the rest of Tuesday evening talking with his Majority Leader and Whip about any delegation shifts—looking at small states with only one member. Most of these states were Republican and his Whip assured him they were firmly supporting their party's nominee. However, there were possible switches in two small states, Delaware and Vermont, held by a Democrat and an independent, respectively.

The Speaker knew the moderate Democratic Congresswoman from Delaware well and was certain she would not flip. However, the independent member from Vermont did not have strong party ties. The Speaker called to see if he could persuade him to switch his vote. However, after an exchange of pleasantries, the Vermont Congressman made it clear he was not budging.

So, the Speaker's attention turned to Michigan and Velvet's no-show during the Tuesday voting. She looked like the best shot for resolving this matter and directed his staff to find her.

"No matter where I am or what I am doing, when you get her on the line, put her through to me. We need to resolve this election quickly, and LeBlanc may be our ticket out of here. Her party dumped her in their primary, so she might be ripe for revenge."

Meanwhile, Velvet spent Tuesday evening in her Soo casino hotel room on a conference call to Wenonah, Tom, and Amy, with Taylor sitting next to her.

Now she felt was the time to make the deal of a lifetime for her vote.

Wenonah urged her to call the White House again and press for an earlier resolution of the barrels issue. As Velvet pondered making the call, there was a knock on her door. When Taylor answered it, he was met by the hotel manager, who apologized for the interruption.

"I know you asked not to be disturbed, but the White House and the Speaker's office both said it was urgent," the manager explained. He then handed Taylor the written phone messages with return phone numbers.

Taylor thanked him and brought the messages to Velvet.

"How in the world did they both find me so fast?" Velvet asked.

"Well, whatever, we have to speed up our discussions, as I fear it will not be long before the press finds us as well," Taylor advised.

Then Velvet noticed on the note that the White House call was not from the chief of staff but the President himself.

The President is calling? OMG!

"I'm sorry but I'm going to have to call you all back, as I have some urgent calls to return," Velvet said, ending her telephone conference call.

She then turned to Taylor.

"I'm calling the President right now. I wonder what he might offer that his Chief of Staff didn't," she said, smiling as she dialed the number. She put the call on speaker so Taylor could hear the conversation.

The call went through, and a female voice said, "Hold for the President."

Then a deep voice intoned, "Congresswoman LeBlanc, how are you doing? My staff say you prefer to be called Velvet. May I call you Velvet?" he asked.

"Certainly, Mr. President," Velvet replied. "And I am doing well, considering the circumstances."

"Good, good. Well, Velvet, I just have a few minutes. But as you know, the House is trying to determine who my successor will be and is in a bit of a bind. I talked to the Speaker just a few minutes ago, and he tells me you can resolve this thing for us. I assume you'll be voting when the House reconvenes on Thursday, right?"

"Yes, Mr. President, it is my intention to vote, weather permitting."

"Well, I have a little plane to get you here if you need it."

"Thank you, sir, but as long as Gitche Gumee doesn't object, I'll be there."

There was a pause as the President seemed unfamiliar with the name, but he then turned to Velvet's letter about the Corps.

"My Chief of Staff told you I ordered an investigation of the incident, and I will be happy to put that commitment in writing to you. But though I would like to name you to a task force to explore any of their recommendations, I have two problems."

Velvet waited in silence for the expected continuing equivocation.

"First, the follow-up task force may or may not be necessary after the investigation is concluded, and that will be a decision for the next President, not me."

Velvet again said nothing.

"Second, the investigation might uncover some highly classified information that can't be released to the public. So, cries of a cover-up are likely, harming the credibility of everyone on the task force—including you if you are on it."

Velvet's face flushed in frustration at his words. Was the President walking back on the commitment of his Chief of Staff, using national security as his justification for not creating a task force or appointing her to it?

"What national security issues could possibly arise from dumping contaminated material into Lake Superior?" Velvet asked.

The President did not elaborate, but he promised Velvet he would "do right" by her on the issue and assured her that the Republican nominee was sympathetic to his task force commitment.

"That is, if you vote for her and she becomes President," he added.

Then he excused himself for another meeting and hung up.

Velvet turned to Taylor and asked him what he thought of the President's 'commitment' on the Corps issue.

Taylor frowned and recommended that she contact the Republican nominee to see if she were indeed on board with the Corps investigation and task force idea.

Velvet agreed and asked Taylor to find and contact her.

In the meantime, Velvet called the Speaker to determine whether the House and Senate deadlock had changed his previous contingent offer of committee assignments.

Her call went through directly to the Speaker, who skipped his usual pleasantries and jumped to his reason for calling: "Are you going to be on the House floor on Thursday when the House reconvenes, and have you decided who you will support?"

There was a pause, as Velvet did not respond right away.

He continued. "Velvet, the House leadership is in a bind, and we need your vote," he explained.

Finally, he addressed me by my first name and now seems more accommodating than in our previous conversation, she thought to herself.

"Yes, I plan to be there on Thursday, but I need to take the oath of office before the House reconvenes."

The Speaker immediately agreed and offered to administer the oath in his office.

Then Velvet reiterated her request for committee assignments, reminding him that in their last conversation he couldn't guarantee her a seat on either of her two committee choices.

The Speaker responded that IF she were to join the Republican caucus, he would personally support a position for her on BOTH committees.

His promise delighted Velvet, but she continued to press her second issue: had he talked to the President about the Corps investigation as he had promised earlier, and was he supportive of forming a task force to review the findings? And would he support her as co-chair of such a task force?

The Speaker stammered and said he had talked to the White House Chief of Staff about the task force issue and would be on board with the idea and her role on it, but it would only happen if the Republican nominee were President.

It's about time I received a direct response, she thought.

She then thanked the Speaker and assured him she was pleased with his response.

However, recognizing showing her cards now would end her negotiating ability, she found another angle to delay her announcement. She told him she needed to talk to the two presidential nominees prior to making her final decision to assess their level of commitment to the Corps' investigation.

The Speaker agreed such meetings were fair and urged her to call him anytime about any concerns after her conversations, giving her his personal cell number.

Mission accomplished, she thought.

After she ended her call with the Speaker, Taylor had found the Republican Presidential nominee, who was awaiting Velvet's return call.

"Give me a second, Taylor. I want to savor this moment."

To buy another day so she could negotiate with other political figures, she invited both Presidential nominees to meet with her immediately after she took the oath of office on Thursday. Only then she would announce her decision.

Both party nominees agreed to meet at Velvet's congressional office in the Longworth Building on Thursday morning, prior to the House re-convening to continue the voting process.

Then, before retiring for the night, she decided it was time to negotiate with two other political figures: Michigan's Republican Governor and the House Minority Leader.

Her call to the Governor focused on the Line 5 issue. She wanted a commitment that he would publicly and in writing support legislation now pending in the state legislature to terminate the line 5 underwater easement that the state had granted almost 75 years ago. She stressed the word "public," as she learned from her last encounter with the Governor that she needed to be specific so he couldn't squirm out of the commitment.

The Governor tried to hedge on this, saying it would depend on the ultimate form of the legislation, but Velvet persisted. This was a non-negotiable demand, and she would not vote with the Republicans in the Michigan congressional delegations if he did not agree to support easement termination.

After several minutes of negotiation, he agreed to her demand and texted her his commitment, which was to be released only if there was a Republican President.

Then, she called the House Democratic Minority Leader. Let me see what he can offer, she thought.

He was eager to talk to her and reminisced about his fond memories with Joe, but Velvet cut him off.

"We both know the party abandoned me after my special election victory. Joe's party, your party, my party—all of you worked behind my back to recruit Lorraine."

"And for me," she continued, "I received no party financial support, no decent committee assignments, and no support for my legislation. Why, in God's name, should I listen to this drivel about your love for Joe after such treatment?"

The Minority Leader listened without comment as Velvet continued.

"I realize I did not fit into your Washington society, a First American woman from rural Michigan, but you could at least have given me some personal support. But no, you ignored me. And now you expect me to support your nominee for President?"

The Minority Leader, sensing that Velvet had finished venting, replied in measured tones.

"We ask you to join us and support our nominee because you know in your heart that the Democratic Party is in your soul and was in the soul of your late husband." Then, he interjected a litany of questions:

"You care about the environment—but do you really think the Republicans will suddenly become green if you vote for their nominee?

"Do you think the mining interests who supported the Republican Party will stop polluting because of your vote for their nominee?

"You care about your Native American culture. Yet how do you justify supporting the Republican candidate's running mate, who constantly belittles minorities?

"Do you want the Republicans to control both Houses of Congress and the Presidency? Do you realize how this country will suffer if the one percent and their Republican allies go unchecked as they were after the 2016 election?

"Velvet, look deep into your heart and don't be fooled by Republican promises when they need you. You know they will promise you anything until they get your vote."

His words moved Velvet.

The Democratic Party had always been the keeper of her dreams and principles. Her launchpad into politics with Joe was the Democratic Party. Maybe she was being seduced by the illusory promises of the Republican Party.

When she hung up, her face betrayed her indecision.

Taylor smiled and said, "Sleep on it."

Velvet nodded and walked from the living area of the hotel suite to the bedroom, as Taylor returned to his room.

This was one night she would never forget.

CHAPTER SEVENTEEN

The Path Forward

"A typical vice of American politics is the avoidance of saying anything real on real issues."

—Theodore Roosevelt

SAULT STE. MARIE, MICHIGAN
WEDNESDAY, JANUARY 8, 2024

VELVET AWOKE EARLY WEDNESDAY MORNING TO THE RINGING OF HER hotel telephone. It was the casino hotel manager again, calling to tell her that a mob of reporters was waiting in the lobby for her to emerge.

She looked out the hotel room window and saw a bustling casino parking lot. The sparsely populated lot was now teeming with local media vehicles, transforming what was an early morning homogenous white wilderness into a grimy, gray mass of dirty snow defiled by the tire tracks of incoming press vehicles.

Velvet needed an escape plan to avoid the reporters. She didn't want to slip up and tip her hand to the press on her presidential vote nor further alienate the press by more evasive answers. Amy had arranged a morning breakfast meeting with the Sault tribal council, but that was before the press learned of Velvet's whereabouts. Velvet texted Amy to reschedule their meeting for a later date.

She went to Taylor's room, softly tapping on his door.

He opened the door, obviously just awakened, wearing only an old CMU jersey and cutoffs.

"May I come in?" Velvet asked.

"Of course, Velvet."

Closing the door behind her, she got right to the point.

"Taylor, we have a problem. I need to leave the hotel and avoid the reporters who are waiting downstairs. What can we do? The hotel manager says they have taken over the lobby."

Taylor rubbed his eyes and thought for a moment.

"Let me make a call that I think might fix this situation," he responded after a long pause.

He pulled up the contact list on his cell phone. Finding the Governor's office phone number, he plunked down on his bed, phone in hand.

"I'd like to call the Governor's office and find out when his plane is arriving to pick you up this morning. When it lands, I'll ask them to send a limo to the casino entrance, but the limo should wait only TEN minutes. If we don't appear by then, we will have found another way to the airport and the limo should leave."

"How does that get me on the plane?" Velvet asked.

"I'll tell Amy to disclose to the press that the Governor is sending a limo to pick you up at the casino entrance. That will lure the reporters away from the hotel lobby."

"Then what?" Velvet asked.

"When the reporters rush to that casino entrance as the limo pulls up, I will be sitting nearby in a rental car and text you to come down to the hotel lobby. I'll meet you in the lobby carport, which the press will have deserted, and take you to the airport."

"Sounds like a good plan, Taylor. Do it."

Taylor called the Governor's office and confirmed that the limo would pick them up at 9:30 am. He then emailed Amy to leak the limo pickup time to the press and Velvet's planned departure on the Governor's plane.

The plan worked almost as Taylor projected, and Velvet slipped out the lobby door, avoiding the throng of reporters waiting at the casino entrance when the limo arrived.

However, the two local reporters who had pushed the sex scandal story decided that rather than fighting the swarm of reporters at the casino, it would be smarter to go to the airport in Kinross where the Governor's plane would land. There, they could separate Velvet from the other reporters and get the personal interview they wanted.

When Velvet and Taylor arrived at the Chippewa County International Airport in Kinross, the two reporters were waiting for them in the parking lot. They approached her car just as she and Taylor stepped out. What followed was a cascade of questions:

"Congresswoman LeBlanc, rumor has it you were offered a cabinet position if you vote for the Democratic nominee. Is that true?"

"What are the Republicans offering you if you support their nominee?"

"Did the Governor promise to shut down Line 5 if you supported the Republican nominee?"

"What do you hope to learn from your meetings with the Republican and Democratic Presidential nominees on Thursday?"

"Can you forgive the Democratic Party for not supporting you in the August primary and for the Democratic Party chair sleeping with your husband?"

"Are you still sleeping with your aide?" one reporter asked, pointing to Taylor.

Velvet and Taylor continued to walk towards the small terminal where the Governor's Chief of Staff was waiting and ignored all but the last question.

The personal nature of her relationship with Taylor struck a sensitive nerve. Rather than deny or ignore that personal allegation, she responded instinctively.

"Even if I were, what business is that of yours?"

She then turned back and rejoined Taylor, who winced at her comment. Silence was the better course of action. Responding without making an out-right denial could be construed as an admission, he worried.

Meanwhile, the reporters had their story and rushed to push their new sex angle.

Velvet and Taylor walked briskly to the terminal where the Chief of Staff waited. They were then escorted to the Governor's plane, which immediately departed for Washington.

Velvet and Taylor sat together on the plane as the Chief of Staff casually talked about her upset election win and the Governor's help with her special election victory. He broached the subject of the House vote and reminded her that the Democrats had rebuffed her in the primary.

"You know, Velvet, you would be very welcome in the Republican Party after that shoddy treatment from your party. We could work together over the Governor's last two years to address the issues you hold so dear, including Line 5 and mining pollution. You would have a much more sympathetic ear of the Governor if you were in our party."

Velvet did not respond right away, as she had heard illusory promises from the Governor before. However, she pressed him on the Line 5 issue.

"Are you saying the Governor would guarantee to shut down Line 5 ONLY IF I joined the Republican Party?"

"No, I am just saying that the Governor would listen more closely to a Republican member of Congress from the First District than a Democrat," he replied. "I can't speak for the Governor. I'm just stating the obvious."

"Well, I've told the Governor I want a clear, public statement from him supporting the decommissioning of Line 5, and he has agreed. I may be a relative newcomer to the political world, but I have at least learned that lesson."

Velvet then waved off further conversation and said she needed to rest.

However, the Chief of Staff made one last poke: "So have you decided how you are going to vote on the Presidency yet?"

Velvet smiled and closed her eyes. She was not revealing her cards to him, of all people.

When the plane landed at the Ronald Reagan Washington National Airport Wednesday morning, Velvet and Taylor thanked the Chief of Staff for the ride and disembarked. However, after she arrived at the gate and towards a staffer who was waiting to pick her up, she found a mob of national press reporters waiting for her.

The word was out, and Velvet was now in the national political spotlight.

Passing through the wall of reporters, she saw a familiar face: Rachel Maddow!

OMG, she thought, Rachel is here, and she's waving at me!

Rather than fleeing the reporters, she turned and walked towards Maddow, much to the chagrin of Taylor, who was trying to guide her out of the airport terminal without comments to the press.

"Representative LeBlanc, have you decided who you are going to support for President of the United States?" inquired Maddow with a camera rolling behind her.

Velvet shook her head no.

"When will you make that decision?"

"Soon," Velvet responded with a smile.

"Can we assume that since you arrived in a Republican Governor's plane that you are leaning towards the Republicans?"

Velvet smiled but did not respond.

"Will you come on my show after this vote is over and explain your reasoning?" Maddow asked.

Velvet smiled and said, "Absolutely."

Then, ignoring other reporters' questions, Taylor guided Velvet out of the terminal and into her car for a ride to her congressional office.

Velvet's car ride to her Longworth Building office was tense, as she sat silently while Taylor talked on the phone to Amy and Wenonah, seeking details on the day's events. Upon arrival at her congressional office, Amy ushered her into her personal office and, together with Wenonah, outlined the schedule for the next day.

Amy had scheduled her first meeting on Thursday at 9:30 am, when she and Wenonah would accompany Velvet to the Speaker's office to take the oath of office. The Speaker also might describe the House procedures for the vote and talk about committee assignments, Amy added. The latter issue would, of course, be a backdoor way of determining whether Velvet would join the Republican caucus and support their nominee.

"Don't worry Amy, I can navigate that trap. "

Amy then scheduled Velvet to meet the Democratic nominee at 10:45 in her Longworth office, followed by the Republican nominee at 11:15.

"Only 30 minutes each?" Velvet exclaimed.

"That should be more than enough time to address your issues," Wenonah interjected.

"Wenonah," Velvet interrupted, "I want more time. I can finally have my voice and policies heard by those in a position to implement them. I don't want to be rushed."

"How much time to you need, Velvet? Remember, the House reconvenes at noon, so there is only a brief window of time."

"The House will have some procedural issues and leadership statements, so it is not as though the House will vote precisely at noon. I want an hour with each candidate. So, please advise the nominees and the Speaker of this change in timing."

Amy nodded and left to let the candidates know of this change. Wenonah frowned but also agreed to Velvet's wish and called the Speaker's office.

In the meantime, Velvet relished her newly found prominence. It was exciting to dictate the timing of such an important event.

How often does a Member of Congress interview candidates for the Presidency, she thought gleefully?

After signing some routine paperwork and issuing some staff instructions, she had a staff member drive her to her Virginia apartment to rest and prepare for the monumental day ahead.

Finally, a restful night's sleep, she thought.

CHAPTER EIGHTEEN

Meet the Candidates

"Some men change their party for the sake of their principles;
others their principles for the sake of their party."

—Winston Churchill

WASHINGTON, D.C.
THURSDAY, JANUARY 9, 2025

IT WAS MID-MORNING WHEN VELVET ARRIVED AT HER LONGWORTH Building office, contemplating the momentous events ahead. Amy and Wenonah met her at the office door and advised her it was time to head to the Speaker's Office for the brief oath of office ceremony.

"One minute, please, I need to gather my thoughts," Velvet said.

Looking out her window at the sunny winter morning landscape of Washington, it was going to be a bright new day on her political journey.

As they headed out of her office and down the hallway, the trio had to thread their way through a noisy mob of reporters. Shouting questions as she marched down the hall, reporters looked surprised at the serenity that Velvet exuded. She no longer had the deer in the headlights look of a first year member of Congress, but rather the demeanor of a seasoned politician.

On her subway ride to the Capitol and the Speaker's office, Amy described the abbreviated ceremony in the Speaker's office. Wenonah interjected she had just learned the Speaker had invited the seven Republican Congressmen from Michigan to attend as well.

Clever, thought Velvet. The Speaker has given his party another shot at persuading me to vote for their nominee.

"Thanks for the heads up, Wenonah, but that won't affect me. None of them ever supported me in the first place, and I have no expectation that this meeting will change their views of me in the future."

Upon arriving at the Speaker's office, she had to squeeze her way through a cluster of reporters blocking the entrance. The Speaker had the Capitol Police escort Velvet, Wenonah, and Amy into his reception area and then into his personal office. There stood a small throng of Michigan Republican Congressmen surrounding the Speaker.

The Speaker warmly greeted the three women and pointed to the Michigan Congressmen in the room, whom he said were eager to have her join their delegation. They all heartily applauded her.

Velvet smiled and thanked them for their attendance. She then turned to the Speaker and said she wanted a few words with him in private after the ceremony.

He nodded and, sensing an important moment was at hand, directed everyone to take their places as he administered the oath of office. She remembered the oath well from the first time she took it in April, but now she swore the oath as Velvet, not as Evangeline.

"I, Velvet LeBlanc, do solemnly swear that I will support and defend the Constitution of the United States against all enemies, foreign and domestic; that I will bear true faith and allegiance to the same; that I take this obligation freely, without any mental reservation or purpose of evasion, and that I will well and faithfully discharge the duties of the office on which I am about to enter. So, help me God."

But she felt the oath seemed different this time. It seemed more like a meaningless word salad than a solemn commitment, as she had seen the true colors of those who had taken it. Did they honestly embrace the sacred obligation that the oath represented?

She thought not.

After repeating the oath, shaking hands, and accepting applause and congratulations from those in attendance, Velvet asked Amy and Wenonah to wait outside. She was ready to make this deal with the Speaker by herself.

The Speaker told everyone that he had some paperwork for Velvet to sign and directed his staff to escort everyone else out of the office.

The Speaker then signaled to his assistant to close the door.

"OK, Velvet. What can we expect from you today? Are you with us?"

Velvet paused, recognizing the backhanded message he was sending about her vote. Without responding to his question, she reiterated her understanding of what the Speaker was promising her.

"So, I understand you will support my committee assignments on the Appropriations and Natural Resources Committees, you will support efforts to create a task force to investigate the Corps dumping, and you and the Republican Party will not support the former Republican Congressman from my district should he choose to run in 2026, right?"

"If we have a Republican President and you join our caucus, yes, those are my commitments."

"And if they create a task force, would you support me co-chairing it?"

"Yes, yes, he replied impatiently. Now, can I assume we can count on your vote this afternoon?"

Velvet nodded affirmatively with one caveat: "Unless my meeting with the two nominees this morning uncovers something important that I had not considered."

The Speaker looked pained. But he accepted her qualified statement, nodded, and bid her goodbye.

"I'll see you on the floor soon. I understand from your staff that you may be a little late. There are several procedural issues we need to resolve before we take another vote, so that should be fine."

Velvet thanked him and rejoined Amy and Wenonah in the reception area. Amy arranged for the Capitol Police to escort Velvet back to her office for her appointments, as the media had otherwise blocked her path.

On her way back to her office, she heard questions shouted by reporters about what the Speaker had offered her, which she ignored. However, one question shouted gave her pause.

"Are you still sleeping with that CMU football player?"

Velvet paused and looked at Amy, who explained that *The Sault Evening News* had just published a front-page article about her purported relationship with Taylor. The two reporters had used her evasive response at the airport to expand upon their previous sexual allegation story.

I hate this place, she thought, but kept walking to the subway. Her ride back to the Longworth building was a silent one, as Velvet felt wounded that this untrue story was clouding her day of triumph.

When she arrived at her office at 10:15, the Democratic Presidential nominee and his chief of staff were already waiting for her, fifteen minutes early.

Velvet explained to the nominee that she needed a few minutes before they could meet. I may be putting the next President on hold, she thought.

Huddling with Taylor, Tom, Wenonah, and Amy in her office, they reviewed a list of issues they wanted the Democratic Presidential nominee to address:

1. His position on an investigation into the Corps dumping in Lake Superior.

2. His position on creating a Corps task force and Velvet co-chairing it.

3. His pledge to protect tribal casino regional monopolies.

4. His pledge to investigate the health and environmental effects of mining pollution.

Velvet added two issues that had occurred to her during her flight that morning:

5. His promise to dump Connie as the Michigan Democratic party chair because of her affair with Joe.

6. His pledge not to support any primary opponent who runs against her, should she seek re-election in 2026.

Settling upon these six issues and having staff quickly amend the initial typed list, Velvet walked out to the reception area and invited the Democratic nominee and his chief of staff to join them in her office.

After exchanging pleasantries, Velvet thanked the Democratic nominee for agreeing to a longer meeting and presented him with her list of six issues. The nominee glanced at the list and agreed to support both the investigation of the dumping and creating a task force to handle any remediation costs. He also said he would support her co-chairing a task force if one was necessary after the investigation concluded.

As to tribal casino protection, he directed his aide to hand Velvet a thick envelope.

"In that envelope, you will find resolutions from all the federally recognized tribes in your district who endorse my candidacy. That should show my support for tribal casinos, as most of these tribes operate casinos."

Velvet opened the envelope, glancing through the names of tribes. She was impressed.

"As to the mining pollution issue, here is a letter signed by nine local and statewide Michigan environmental organizations ranging from the Michigan Environmental Council to Clean Water Action endorsing my candidacy. My administration will certainly make mining pollution a priority issue."

Again, Velvet was impressed. But after remarking about the importance of the endorsements, she turned to several personal concerns.

"Now there is Connie, the Michigan Democratic Party Chair. I believe she had an affair with my late husband, so I cannot be a member of a party where she will be my key link to state Democrats."

"Understood," said the nominee. "I will find a place for her out of your sight. Anything else?"

"One more thing, about 2026 …"

"Don't worry, that primary challenge mess will not happen again. As head of our party, I personally will assure you of that."

Then the nominee went off the list and made a tantalizing offer.

"Velvet, I would also like you to know that your commitment to Native American issues has impressed me. After the Corps investigation is complete, I would like to nominate you to head the Bureau of Indian Affairs. I think you could do so much more to help Native Americans in that position than as one of 435 members of Congress."

The offer surprised Velvet and intrigued her as well. She thanked him and said she would think about it.

Brilliant, she thought. He flipped his interview into one interviewing her.

Velvet was pleased with his responses and adjourned the meeting after only thirty-five minutes. After the Democratic nominee left, the five sat down and analyzed his responses.

Wenonah started with the obvious. It will be a Republican House and Senate, so the ability to get anything done legislatively without Republican support was unlikely, whether it be mining pollution prevention or casino protection issues.

"True," said Velvet, "but it is unlikely that Republicans would support my legislation whether I was a Democrat or Republican."

The staff nodded in agreement.

Then there is the Corps issue, which Amy pointed out was within the control of the President. He could order a Corps investigation and create an executive branch task force, with Velvet being at least a co-chair. In fact, the more environmentally friendly policies of the Democratic nominee might make the Corps' investigation more thorough and less likely to be constrained by national security roadblocks.

"The Democratic nominee would also be in the best position to deliver on the personal concerns I have with Connie and stopping another primary backstabbing," Velvet added.

"And," she continued, "it was a huge plus that he has the support of both the tribes and the environmental groups in my district—two of my key constituencies."

And then there was the Bureau of Indian Affairs offer.

"What a powerful voice I could have in that post!" she exclaimed.

They all agreed.

There were still fifteen minutes before the Republican nominee was due when they concluded their analysis of the Democratic nominee, so Velvet asked everyone to leave except Wenonah. When they were alone and the office door closed, she posed her question: "Should I take the BIA post if offered, and what would that mean to my staff and supporters?"

"Velvet, you have to do what you think is best not only for the district but also for what you want to do next. You know you will have enemies in the House when you return, no matter who you vote for. Do you really want to face that again, or do you want to take a new path to realize your goals serving in the executive branch?"

"Good point," Velvet replied, nodding in agreement.

She then walked to her door and opened it, calling for Tom.

Tom came in and Velvet told him to close the door.

"Tom, does the Senate have to approve nominees to head the BIA?"

Tom looked surprised at her question. He nodded yes.

Velvet's face dropped, as she knew there was no way a Republican Senate would approve her nomination if she voted for the Democratic nominee.

"Anything else, Velvet? Tom asked.

Velvet shook her head no, and a long period of silence ensued.

She was still thinking about the BIA option when her receptionist buzzed and announced that the Republican nominee and her aide were now waiting in the outer office.

Oh, if my parents could see me now, she thought. What a political high this is!

She wanted to organize her thoughts before the next interview and also enjoy this unique moment.

Velvet buzzed her receptionist and asked that Tom, Amy, Wenonah, and Taylor return to her office before meeting with the Republican nominee. After the five were reunited and strategically placed around her desk, Velvet arose and opened her office door, welcoming in the nominee.

Unlike the Democratic nominee, an average-looking man dressed in a traditional blue suit and red tie, the Republican nominee was a striking woman dressed in an elegant black business suit. She was a tall woman with a milky white complexion and a slender build, who walked with a self-assurance and confidence that impressed Velvet.

Rather than take a seat after greeting Velvet, the nominee walked around the room, greeting each staffer individually and asking how long each had worked in Washington. It was only then that she took a seat next to her aide.

Velvet handed the nominee the original list of four issues. But the nominee seemed already aware of them, as she glanced at the list and nodded her agreement.

"Velvet, I have already talked to the President about the Corps investigation and task force co-chair points, and I am on board with both. As to the mining pollution issue—I can promise that I will appoint heads of the Interior Department and the EPA who are familiar with your concerns—and I will give you an opportunity to interview them personally before publicly announcing my nominees."

She paused and then continued.

"As to tribal casino issues, I am not sure I can support protectionist legislation, but I will promise to convene a White House conference on tribal gaming within the first two years of my term and designate you as a keynote speaker to present your point of view."

Her answers did not fully satisfy Velvet, but Velvet pressed on.

"What about your vice president? I have profound disagreements with him on both environmental and tribal policy issues?"

"Can we speak alone?" the nominee asked.

Velvet agreed and signaled for everyone to leave. When the room emptied and her office door closed, the nominee asked that what she was about to say be kept confidential.

Velvet nodded in agreement.

The nominee first noted the tie vote in the Senate for the Vice Presidency and felt the deadlock might resolve the vice president problem for them both. She related how the vice-presidential nominee was forced upon her, as Tom had speculated, and how she had serious disagreements with him on some major issues.

"Velvet, the Twenty-fifth Amendment is our savior. Under Section 2, if the Senate does not resolve the tie and leaves the vice president position vacant, it empowers me if I become President to nominate someone else who needs confirmation only by a majority of both houses of Congress. And my party will have that majority in both houses."

She continued, "It is my intention to declare the vice president seat vacant upon being selected President, and then I will find a running mate more in tune with your views and mine."

"Do you think the Senate will remain deadlocked?"

"Yes, my running mate has made many powerful enemies on both sides of the aisle, so there will be no defections or mourning for his demise."

"And what about 2026, if I decide to run for re-election?"

"I can't promise you a pass, but I will pledge that neither I nor any member of my administration will campaign against you in your district."

With that, she offered a personal observation.

"Velvet, whatever you decide, I'm glad it will be a woman who decides my fate."

Velvet smiled and then rose to invite the staff members back into her office. They all entered and returned to their original seats, wondering if she would brief them on the private conversation that had just occurred.

However, Velvet had no intention of betraying that confidence, and asked them whether they had questions for the nominee.

No one asked another question.

Velvet then stood and thanked the Republican nominee for her candor.

The candidate rose and, wishing Velvet well, left the room with her aide.

Velvet signaled to Tom to close the door. She then asked everyone for their thoughts about what they had just heard.

Wenonah started, pointing out that the Republican nominee had dodged the environmental and First American issues.

Tom noted it was unlikely any meaningful legislation on these two subjects would pass anyway, since conservative Republicans would control both houses of Congress. Getting a say on the EPA and DOI nominees and a White House conference on tribal casinos was as good a deal as she could expect from a Republican.

"But all that is just talk and no action," Velvet fretted.

Taylor pointed to the promise of a task force chair and an investigation as promising developments. However, Velvet also noted it was the same promise that the Democratic nominee offered.

There was no offer of a job in the new Administration nor a pledge not to support a strong challenger against her in 2026, but Tom observed that such an offer would be politically unwise even if Velvet became a Republican, as it would look too much like a quid pro quo.

"What did she say about her VP?" Tom asked.

"It appears the Senate is deadlocked, so it's an open question of how this will be resolved," she replied evasively.

Velvet then asked everyone to leave except Wenonah.

"It's almost 12:30, and the House is already in session, so you need to get to the floor as soon as possible," Amy reminded her as she was leaving.

"In due time," Velvet replied. "In due time."

"Let me have this last moment with my sister."

CHAPTER NINETEEN

Destiny

*"Fame comes only when deserved, and then is as
inevitable as destiny, for it is destiny."*

—Henry Wadsworth Longfellow

VELVET WALKED BACK TO HER DESK AND FELL INTO HER LEATHER CHAIR,
slouching and staring out her Capitol Hill office window. Wenonah plopped
down beside her on a nearby chair and waited for Velvet to broach the question that was clearly vexing her.

"Is this what political victory feels like?" Velvet asked Wenonah.

Wenonah just smiled.

"Is this the ultimate high that politicians so lust for: exercising political power and having your friends and foes curry your favor?"

Again, Wenonah did not respond.

"Should I even be here if it means I will have to become just as manipulative as they are to be successful?"

Wenonah made sure Velvet was finished with her litany of concerns before offering her assessment.

"You have suffered so many misfortunes and indignities in your political journey, but you also have learned a key lesson. There is no ultimate political victory, no long-lasting solution to any policy issue. Politics is only a continuing series of battles and compromises—of victories and defeats. In the end, you only lose when you are not true to yourself and your principles."

Velvet looked at her sister, recognizing the wisdom of her words. She took no great solace in making her upcoming decision, somewhat fearful of the political consequences of her vote.

However, Wenonah's words comforted her, knowing that whatever decision she made, it would not be the end of the world.

Wenonah reminded her she was eating the forbidden political fruit that her parents had been denied. And she had achieved a political position of power to which Joe had aspired but never achieved.

"Mother and Father would be so proud of you, Velvet," Wenonah said lovingly.

Velvet harkened back to her time as a child with her parents. This was indeed the taste of victory that they had never enjoyed. Gitche Gumee had given that honor to her alone.

She smiled and reflexively stroked her neck, reaching for her locket with her parents' picture in it, but then recalled she had left it at Abequa's spirit house. It was where it needed to be, she thought.

Despite his unforgivable infidelity, she also wondered what Joe would have thought about her pending decision. Unlike her, he had always wanted to be in the political limelight, but the waves of Gitche Gumee dashed this quest, too.

Then, she thought about the barrels that Gitche Gumee belched onto its shores—the event that gave her a political opportunity that neither Joe nor her parents had.

It now seemed clear that the trials and tribulations that Lake Superior had heaped on her had served as a catalyst for this moment, her wild ride down a tortuous political path. The arms of Gitche Gumee had guided her down a less traveled path, using its powerful waves not to punish her but to burnish her political skills in preparation for this very moment.

She was about to cast the most momentous vote that any single member of Congress had ever taken. She took a deep breath, her heart pounding with excitement.

Just then, there was a sharp knock on the door, startling both Velvet and Wenonah. It was Amy, and she did not wait for a reply before bursting into Velvet's private office.

She was in an extreme state of agitation.

"Amy, I asked to be alone with my sister for a few moments. Can't whatever you have to tell me wait?"

"No, it can't!" Amy responded, ashen faced. "I just got a call from a *Washington Post* reporter who claims to have a transcript of your recent telephone conversation with the President. He said the President offered you a bribe if you voted for the Republican nominee. He wants your comment before they post the transcript on their website today."

"How did they get a transcript? Is it genuine? Who could have released it and why?" Velvet shouted in quick succession.

"Only you would know if it's genuine. Who recorded it and why is irrelevant at this moment?" Amy responded.

"Well, what's the big deal? Aren't deals cut all the time to get things done in Congress? The press reported many offers were being made to the lumberjack candidate for his vote."

"Yes, but the offers were never verified, and he didn't accept any of them," Amy replied.

"Well, I have been offered prime committee assignments by the Speaker and cabinet positions or reelection help if I vote for a particular candidate. How is this any different from the President offering to investigate a threat to Gitche Gumee?" Velvet asked.

"Velvet, the President is quoted in a written transcript as agreeing to an investigation of the Corps and a task force chair position for you explicitly in exchange for your vote for the Republican nominee. Other offers to you occurred in private; this one was recorded and involves the President of the United States."

Velvet frowned but did not respond.

"Is that excerpt accurate?" Amy asked.

"Yes."

"Velvet, don't you see the political implications of this conversation? If the President did indeed promise you the task force chair in exchange for your vote for the Republican nominee, the nominee would have to disavow the agreement or be complicit in the deal."

"So, this is not about the deal itself, but because it's recorded. Is that the problem?" Velvet asked.

"Precisely. It is one thing for critics and the press to allege offers were made for your vote, but no candidate would confirm such offers because of their quid pro quo implications. However, a recorded conversation is a smoking gun that can't be ignored and may well trigger a full-scale investigation of the President, the Republican nominee—and you."

"This is crazy. I was elected to deliver for my constituents, and I am trying to do so, just like Joe did. When I finally got in this position where politicians needed my vote, I offered it in exchange for what my district needed. I got the Governor to agree to shut down Line 5, the Corps' dumping of toxic waste into Gitche Gumee investigated, and my political position improved to pass legislation my constituents need by being placed on the right committees. I thought that was a pretty good deal for everyone. There was no personal gain for me."

"But–"

"But nothing, Amy. When I tried the legislative and regulatory routes, I was shot down. So I chose the route that Gitche Gumee opened up, and now you are saying I was wrong to do so just because it became public? If I were wrong to do so, why aren't others punished as well?"

"Others have been. Don't you remember the jailing of former Illinois Governor Rod Blagojevich for recorded schemes similar to this?" Amy chimed in.

Velvet stumbled back to her chair. She waved Amy away, trying to compose herself while considering the transcript threat.

"Are there criminal implications in my conversation?" Velvet asked.

"Well, if you vote for the Republican nominee and then she appoints you chair of the Corps task force or you accept any of the other 'bribes' that the President and by implication the Republican nominee offered in the transcript, there could be," Amy replied. "We would need a legal opinion to determine that definitively."

"So, what you are saying is that to avoid possible criminal prosecution, I should vote for the Democratic nominee?"

"I am not telling you how to vote. I am just explaining the political and legal baggage that your vote now carries with the release of this transcript," Amy replied.

Wenonah jumped in, arguing that such deals are common and unlikely to result in criminal prosecution. But she agreed that the likely scandalous headlines could lead to painful congressional hearings and an investigation by the Justice Department.

The idea of a confirmation hearing after release of the transcript made any Administration nomination highly unlikely.

"Why did I choose to swim in this amoral political sea? Why?" Velvet asked rhetorically.

Then she paused and composed herself, reflecting upon the larger issue of her parents' mission.

"Amy, call the WAPO reporter back and tell him my response will be my vote on the floor of the House in the next few minutes."

Amy, Wenonah, and Taylor began leaving her office, but Velvet asked Taylor to stay behind for just one more moment. Amy frowned and then exited, slamming the door behind her.

"Taylor, what have I done? Here I am at the height of political power and yet I am staring down into the abyss."

Taylor hugged Velvet.

"You should take comfort in the deals you made to protect Gitche Gumee and your district, and how much you have learned through the adversity of your campaign trail. Remember the old line that 'what doesn't kill you makes you stronger?'"

"Do you think I should vote for the Democrat to avoid possible criminal charges against me?"

"I know you will do the right thing, so trust your heart, Velvet," Taylor responded. "Remember, this is graduation time for you in Washington, and you have finished at the top of your class. You will decide who will become our next President. Seize this moment."

Velvet forced a smile but still looked pained, so Taylor continued.

"Do what you think is true to you and your parents' mission, and let the political consequences fall where they may. This is the time for you to decide what is more important: what you believe is best for your district or what is politically expedient."

Velvet embraced Taylor and kissed him gently on the cheek.

Taylor looked surprised, but then beamed.

"You'd better go," he said. "The political world awaits you."

Velvet nodded and motioned for Taylor to leave. She then walked to her closet where her favorite wrap-around skirt was hanging. She plucked the skirt and blouse out and carried it towards the window, pressing it against her body.

Light white snowflakes were falling as she gazed out her window. The nation's capital was under a snow advisory, and the multi-colored vehicles below would soon become a homogenous and indistinguishable white mass.

White eventually absorbs everything, she observed.

A phone intercom buzz interrupted her quiet introspection. It was her receptionist calling to tell her that the Speaker was on the other line, and it was urgent.

Velvet took the call, and the Speaker jumped to the point: "Velvet, we just finished all the preliminary business and are going to proceed to a vote. I know you have finished meeting with both candidates. I'm going to ask for a quorum call to buy you time to get here, but you must come now."

The Speaker paused. "History awaits you," he added ominously.

"I'm on my way," Velvet replied.

Just then, the bell went off in her office, signaling a quorum call was now underway.

She buzzed her receptionist and told her she needed just two more minutes.

The receptionist warned Velvet that the hallway outside her office was crowded with reporters waiting for her to emerge, so she asked Taylor and Tom to run interference for her as she headed for the House chamber.

When she emerged from her private office, she was wearing the same traditional colorful clothes that she had worn when meeting with the Sault tribe earlier that week, a reminder of her proud heritage. Her First American look surprised her staff, as they had become accustomed to her more traditional Washington attire. But they all stood and applauded.

It was her time, and it was going to be done her way.

With Taylor and Tom leading the way, she marched confidently down the hall to the House subway, amidst shouts from reporters. But she no longer heard the shouts, as her path was now clear.

As they rode on the subway car to the House floor, Tom posed the question that was on everyone's mind: would she vote for the Republican nominee?

"The easy thing to do is to vote the way I have voted throughout my lifetime—as a Democrat," Velvet declared.

She paused, noting the approval in Tom's eyes. Then she continued.

"I accept that I'm in a world of political pragmatists and not a world of idealists. I have learned the value of being both strategic and principled in my decision-making. But let me reverse your question," Velvet continued. "Tell me again why I should not support the Republican nominee—and ignore the criminal prosecution issue in your answer."

Tom looked surprised at the 'criminal' comment, as he had not been privy to the *Washington Post* transcript issue Amy had just presented to Velvet.

Taylor swallowed hard, knowing the criminal issue was a potential career-ending problem for Velvet. So he changed the conversation topic to the impact of voting for the Republican nominee and giving Republicans complete control of both branches of government.

"Remember what happened the last time they had such control," warned Taylor, ignoring the elephant in the room issue of criminal liability.

"Think what it will feel like to be in the majority and get hearings on your legislation if you support the Republican," countered Tom.

"Although the environmental groups and the tribes support the Democratic nominee, being in the Republican majority will improve your chances of passing legislation affecting them," Taylor interjected. "Do you want to make a difference or just a statement?"

On that note, the subway car arrived at the Capitol, and Velvet jumped confidently out of the car and marched towards the House floor. The hallway was awash with lobbyists and reporters, eager to know what the House verdict would be.

She felt euphoric.

Here she was, like the times when crowds called her name at environmental rallies, and she felt the energy of the moment and the spirits of her parents. However, the crowd was not clamoring for Velvet and her singing voice, but for Congresswoman LeBlanc and her political voice.

And today her political voice was all-powerful.

She attempted to squeeze through a path Tom and Taylor had created through the gauntlet of media, lobbyists, and politicians blocking her path to the closed House chamber doors. Along the way, a familiar face caught her eye in this sea of political humanity.

It was Connie!

Drawing upon the spiritual bonds of her parents, whom she felt were now leading her forward, she composed herself as she approached the House chamber doors.

There, she paused and turned around, looking over the throng and honed in on Connie. Noting Connie's quizzical look as their eyes met, Velvet spoke to her in a voice so loud that all in the hallway could hear.

"Today, I have chosen the path less traveled in my political journey."

For a moment, the crowded hallway became deathly quiet, as everyone strained to hear her next words.

Velvet paused again, catching her breath and adding even more drama to this pivotal moment in her political journey.

"What are you going to do, Velvet?" a voice boomed from the throng in front of her, piercing the eerie silence.

"When Congress next convenes," she began, "I look forward to addressing the next President of the United States as 'Madam President.'"

With that pronouncement, she pushed open the double doors, and entered the House chamber—and into the annals of Congressional history.

CHAPTER TWENTY

The Fallout

Presidential Race Decided:

Democrats Cry Foul and Demand Investigation

—2025 *Washington Post* Headline

WASHINGTON, D.C.
JANUARY 9, 2025

A NEWSWIRE STORY CIRCULATING SHORTLY AFTER THE HISTORIC HOUSE
vote electing the Republican nominee as President reported Democrats were
demanding a Justice Department investigation into bribes allegedly given
to Representative Evangeline LeBlanc (I-Mich) in exchange for her decisive
presidential vote.

The former President had left for an extended trip to Europe immediately after the vote was announced and was unavailable for comment. The
newly elected Republican President was asked about the transcript printed

in the *Washington Post* alleging that the former President offered Representative LeBlanc a bribe for her vote. She declined comment, noting that she was not a party to that conversation.

The House Speaker denied giving LeBlanc special treatment, although acknowledging she would caucus with his party. When asked about her committee assignments, he said that would be up to his party members to decide.

Representative LeBlanc's office was contacted for her reaction to a possible DOJ investigation. Her office issued the following brief statement:

"When I took the oath of office and swore to God that I would faithfully discharge my duties as a member of Congress, I also made a spiritual commitment to my parents and my people. I vowed to bring to the corridors of political power the message of my parent's 2007 tribal flotilla: to protect our people, our magnificent lands, and the waters of Gitche Gumee.

Today, that message has been delivered.

My parent's journey is finally completed.

Now I must launch my own political journey to realize their goals.

I believe, working with the new Republican Administration, I can better accomplish my parent's goals and I look forward to working with our new President.

I have sworn to support and defend the U.S. Constitution.

But I also pledge to protect and defend my beloved Gitche Gumee, into whose arms I now commit my body and my soul."